THE BEATITUDES:
A PATHWAY TO THEOSIS

THE BEATITUDES: A PATHWAY TO THEOSIS

by Christopher J. Mertens

Publishers Maxim Hodak & Max Mendor

© 2019, Christopher J. Mertens

© 2019, Orthodox Logos Publishing, The Netherlands

www.orthodoxlogos.com

ISBN: 978-9-49222-408-8
ISBN: 978-1-914337-16-1

This book is in copyright. No part of this publication may be reproduced, stored in a retrieval system or transmitted in any form or by any means without the prior permission in writing of the publisher, nor be otherwise circulated in any form of binding or cover other than that in which it is published without a similar condition, including this condition, being imposed on the subsequent purchaser.

Christopher J. Mertens

THE BEATITUDES:
A PATHWAY TO THEOSIS

ORTHODOX LOGOS PUBLISHING

Contents

Forward 8
Preface 10

Chapter 1:
Introduction 14

Chapter 2:
The Ascent of Moses on Mount Sinai 33

Chapter 3:
Blessed Are the Poor in Spirit 53

Chapter 4:
Blessed Are Those Who Mourn 63

Chapter 5: Blessed Are the Meek 72

Chapter 6:
Blessed Are Those Who Hunger
and Thirst for Righteousness 80

Chapter 7:
Blessed Are the Merciful 87

Chapter 8:
Blessed Are the Pure in Heart 92

Chapter 9:
Blessed Are the Peacemakers 101

Chapter 10:
Participation in the Eighth Day 110

Epilogue 119
Bibliography 122
Book Endorsements 127

To my wife, Rhonda

Forward

Father Deacon Christopher Mertens' thesis on 'THE BEATITUDES: A PATHWAY TO THEOSIS' is an exceptional expose submitted as a Master's thesis to the Faculty of the Antiochian House of Studies, in partial fulfillment of the Master of Arts in Applied Orthodox Theology.
In the Gospel of St. Mark, the Lord says:" Verily I say unto you, that there be some of them that stand here, which shall not taste of death, till they have seen the Kingdom of God come with power." (Mark 9:1). These words enlighten the hearts and minds of those who seek theosis and are in pursuit of the Kingdom of God during the span of their lives. In this regard, Deacon's Mertens' book is received as an attempt to read the Beatitudes in the light of the understanding of the Scriptures; especially the life of Moses the prophet and, elaborated by St. Gregory of Nyssa, the Blessed Augustine, St. John Chrysostom, and other Church Fathers, who used the Beatitudes as a ladder of ascent, leading the faithful to theosis.

Deacon Christopher's book is an attempt to bring together the biblical account with the writings of Church Fathers, enriched by the comments of great theologians such as Vladimir Lossky, Bishop Kallistos of Diokleia, and others who converge harmoniously to 'emphacize the truth that endeavoring to ascend the spiritual summit to ultimate union with God ironically opens limitless horizons' (chapter 2).

ST. Symeon The New Theologian, on the Mystical life, says blessed are those who daily feed on Christ and are cleansed of every stain of both soul and body, and those who have recognized already the divine and have become themselves already sons and co-participants of the resurrection light of the Lord. And here I can humbly and proudly say:

There is no doubt that those who seek knowledge of the Scriptures and the comments of the church fathers will find in this book a path of spiritual ascent that will penetrate the hearts and minds of those who seek spiritual perfection and eternal life.

Thanks to Deacon Christopher for his valuable book and for expressing by the Beatitudes the eternal progress in the journey of the soul to theosis and to the acquisition of virtues (Epilogue).

> V. Rev. Joseph Antypas
> St. George Orthodox Church, Troy, Michigan

Preface

This book is a publication of my master's thesis in Applied Orthodox Theology from the Antiochian House of Studies (AHOS), in partnership with the Saint John of Damascus School of Theology of the University of Balamand. The idea for the thesis topic was borne out of the course work on the mystical theology of the Church. I became convinced of the necessity of incorporating an apophatic approach in acquiring knowledge of God to ensure continual growth in the spiritual life and progress toward the goal of deeper communion with God. At the same time, I kept asking myself, how does one go about developing an apophatic disposition and infuse it into everyday living? How does one consciously go about advancing the soul toward theosis in a concrete way?

As I puzzled over these questions, I suppose it was not too surprising that my thoughts gravitated toward the Beatitudes. After all, for as long as I can remember, I've esteemed the Beatitudes to be the greatest words spoken by our Lord, or ever spoken for that matter. They are music to my heart. I've always had the sense that the Beatitudes are the Gospel, containing all the treasures of the Kingdom of God, just waiting to be found if only one would commit to the task of digging. Serendipitously, I was teaching an adult education series at my parish on the Beatitudes at the same time I was taking the course work on the mystical theology of the Church. I began to study St. Gregory of Nyssa's sermons on the Beatitudes as a source of material for the adult education series I was teaching. I was delighted and greatly encouraged to discover that St. Gregory saw the Beatitudes as a ladder to ascend in the journey of the soul towards mystical union with God, affirming my initial instincts.

The instructional method employed by St. Gregory in his sermons on the Beatitudes is to expound each virtue congratulated, and then provide guidance for the follower of Christ to stretch and expand his soul in the assimilation of the virtues towards union with the infinite glory and goodness of the Holy Trinity. The Beatitudes for St. Gregory provide instructions and guidance for the development of the spiritual life with an apophatic approach that leads to ever-greater participation in the Divine Life. At this point, there was no question of what my thesis topic would be. I had found the answer to the questions I had been asking myself. The answer to my questions is this: It is the Beatitudes that illuminate the path and guide the soul toward theosis in a step-by-step, concrete way.

The goal of this book is to show how each Beatitude opens up boundless opportunities for progress in contemplation and inner purification at each step in the ascent of soul towards union with God. Although the contributions from many Church Fathers and churchmen are included in this work, the primary approach taken to accomplish the goal of this work is to produce a synthesis of the writings of St. John Chrysostom, Blessed Augustin, and St. Gregory of Nyssa. At each step in the ladder of the Beatitudes, St. John Chrysostom illuminates the initial approach to assimilating the virtues expressed in the Beatitudes by identifying and characterizing ways of *putting on Christ*. The apophatic approach to extend beyond the affirmative knowledge of the Beatitudes is revealed most clearly in the writings of St. Gregory of Nyssa. The theological approach of Blessed Augustin falls somewhere in between the literal application of St. John and the mystical theology of St. Gregory. The writings of these three Church Fathers provide the theological core of achieving the objective of this book: - i.e., to show that the Beatitudes provide a pathway to theosis.

The Church is blessed to possess the writings of these three Fathers on the Beatitudes. Each one has a unique, yet complementary, theological vision for growth in the spiritual life. Taken together, the writings from these three Fathers provide a comprehensive view of the pathway to theosis and a trustworthy guide on navigating the soul along its journey to communion with God. St Gregory and Blessed Augustin both saw the Beatitudes as an image of a ladder, by which Christ the Word leads His follower one step at a time towards union with God. Blessed Augustin saw the Beatitudes more as a ladder leading the faithful from the lesser virtues to the more excellent. St. Gregory, whose apophatic approach is more explicit, sees the Beatitudes as a ladder leading to mystical union with God. One does not *see* God's essence, but rather *see*s God by possessing Him within oneself. St. Gregory agrees with Blessed Augustin that the Beatific Vision is achieved by developing the virtues of the soul, especially inner purity and freedom from the passions.

In contrast to St. Gregory and Blessed Augustin, who were heavily influenced by the Alexandrian school of biblical interpretation, St. John Chrysostom is grounded in the Antiochene school of interpretation. Thus, St. John places more emphasis on the literal sense of the biblical text. He sees the Beatitudes as Jesus's commandments to apply to the flesh, and the rewards of such obedience as sensible promises rather than mystical or eschatological promises.

Nevertheless, one can still discern the image of a ladder in the order of the Beatitudes in St. John's interpretation, however obliquely, as his emphasis shifts from the sensible realm to the spiritual realm in proceeding from the first to the last of the Beatitudes.

The foundational background and context of this book for seeing the Beatitudes as a pathway to theosis is provided in the second chapter of this book by summarizing St. Gregory of Nyssa's exegesis of the Book of Exodus in his work entitled *The Life of Moses*. For St. Gregory, the life of Moses is a prophetic symbol of the spiritual journey of the soul to God. The apophatic approach implied by the Beatitudes was prefigured in Moses's ascent of Mount Sinai, which the Church has always associated with the ascent to knowledge of God and union with Him.

I am grateful for the encouragement and feedback from Fr. Joseph Antypas throughout the Doctrine courses of AHOS, and for his encouragement to go forward and pursue this topic for my thesis, which is now being published as a book. I am also thankful for Fr. David Hester for carefully reading the manuscript and identifying several typographical mistakes. Any remaining errors are due to my oversight and negligence.

I am eternally grateful for the love and support of my traveling companion along the journey to God, my wife, Rhonda. There were many occasions when she wished I was spending time with her rather than with my nose in a book or writing my thesis. Her loving sacrifice is more than I deserve.

Chapter 1:
Introduction

Beatitude is the possession of all that is good, from which nothing is absent that a good desire may want[1]. Blessedness is the state of beatitude which is unconditional happiness and contentment. The one thing truly blessed is God Himself, for blessedness is God's way of being. "The Lord God is blessed; blessed is the Lord from day to day" (Ps. 67:19-20 [The Orthodox Study Bible]). The nature of the Godhead is inaccessible and unknowable to the created order (e.g., John 1:18; I John 4:12; I Tim. 6:16). Nevertheless, whatever the Divine Life may be in its ineffable and incomprehensible goodness, it is beatitude. The beatitude of God is an inexpressible beauty, which is very grace, wisdom, and power; it is the true light, which is the fountain of all goodness, and mighty above all else; it is the one thing lovable which is always the same, always rejoicing in infinite happiness[2].

Man is created in the *image* and *likeness* of God (Gen. 1:26-28). Discerning the ways in which man is the image and likeness of God has long been a subject of intense investigation in the writings of the Church Fathers and in

---

[1] St. Gregory of Nyssa, *The Lord's Prayer, The Beatitudes*, trans. Hilda C. Graef, vol. 18, Ancient Christian Writers: The Works of the Fathers in Translation, ed. Johannes Quasten and Joseph C. Plumpe (New York: Paulist Press, 1954), 87.

[2] *Ibid.*, 87.

Scripture itself. According to the Book of Wisdom, "God created man for immortality and made him an image of His own eternity" (Wisd. of Sol. 2:23). The *image* of God is what forms the ontological basis of man's relationship to God[3] (cf. Gen. 2:7). To summarize St. Gregory of Nyssa, "the soul of man is created in the image of God as a mirror reflecting Him."[4] The *likeness* of God is a dynamic realization of the capacity of man to bear the image of God and increase in His divine glory and goodness[5]. As a result, God has sown within each human being all the gifts, in seed-like form, which form us in His image and lead us toward His likeness[6]. Being made in the image and likeness of God (Gen. 1:26-28), man is called to the blessed life (Gen. 2:7-8; 3:8, Ps. 132:3), to the extent that he freely participates in the true beatitude (Eph. 1:3-6; 2 Pet. 1:2-4), as a communicant of divine grace[7].

The Only-Begotten Son, who fashioned man's soul in the likeness of the only Blessed One (Gen. 1:26-28; Col. 1:15-17), describes in the opening words of His Sermon on the Mount all that produces beatitude (Matt. 5:3-10). The beatific form is communion with God, as St. Gregory of Nyssa exclaimed: "The Lord does not say it is blessed to know something about God, but to have God present

---

[3] Norman Russell, *Fellow Workers with God: Orthodox Thinking on Theosis*, Book 5 of the Foundations Series (Crestwood, NY: St. Vladimir's Press, 2009), 91.

[4] Hilda C. Graef, introduction to *The Lord's Prayer, The Beatitudes*, by St. Gregory of Nyssa, 17.

[5] Russell, *Fellow Workers with God: Orthodox Thinking on Theosis*, 91.

[6] Archimandrite Christoforos Stavropoulos, *Partakers of Divine Nature*, trans. Rev. Dr. Stanley Harakas, 6th printing (Minneapolis: Light and Life Publishing, 1976), 26.

[7] *Ibid.*, 17-19.

within oneself." [8]That beatitude is the fulfillment of the divine call of man as the attainment of union with God is made explicit by the Apostle Paul: "To them [the saints] God willed to make known what are the riches of the glory of this mystery [of salvation] among the Gentiles: which is Christ in you, the hope of glory" (Col. 1:27; see also John 14:14-21; 17:3; 20:26). Therefore, the Beatitudes illuminate the pathway to *theosis*[9] ("*deification*" or "*divinization*"), which is a journey of eternal progress in the virtuous life (Matt. 5:48) by which a perpetual transformation is made into the likeness of God "from glory to glory, just as by the Spirit of the Lord" (2 Cor. 3:18).

Theosis is a complex term with both anthropological and economic components. Norman Russell provides a definition that nicely synthesizes the teachings from Scripture and the Church Fathers:

> Theosis is the restoration as persons to integrity and wholeness by participation in Christ through the Holy Spirit, in a process which is initiated in this world through our life of ecclesial communion and moral striving and finds ultimate fulfillment in our union with the Father – all within the broad content of the divine economy[10].

---

8   St. Gregory of Nyssa, *The Lord's Prayer, The Beatitudes*, 148.

9   Christopher Venianmin, *The Orthodox Understanding of Salvation: "Theosis" in Scripture and Tradition* (Dalton, PA: Mount Thabor, 2016), 14, 25. *Theosis* is the *deification* or *divinization* of the entire person in Christ through the union of the human with the divine, to be "partakers of the divine nature" (2 Pet. 1:4) – i.e., participants in the nature of God and in the life of Christ (John 10:25-39; Ps. 81:6). There is an exchange of lives in our souls and bodies with His flesh, His humanity, which is achieved by our ascetic struggles through the grace of the Holy Spirit in the Sacraments of the Church.

10 Russell, *Fellow Workers with God: Orthodox Thinking on Theosis*, 21.

The word theosis is formed from the Greek word *theoo*, which means "to make god"[11]. *Theosis* was first used in the fourth century by St. Gregory of Nazianzus. However, the word *theosis* encompasses an understanding of the purpose and process of man's deification that is traced back to the second century Church Fathers and the New Testament writers themselves. Sts. Clement of Alexandria, Hippolytus of Rome, and Irenaeus of Lyon discussed various aspects of theosis as they reflected on the significance of Christ in the Scriptures. The most frequent biblical texts used by the Church Fathers to support their teaching on deification are: Ps. 81.6, "I said you are gods" and 2 Pet. 1:4, "partakers of divine nature." These passages were consistently quoted from the beginning of the Church as referring to theosis[12]. The quotation from Psalm 81 is much older and the most important. The earliest Christian text to quote this passage is the Gospel of John (John 10:34-36). St. John the Evangelist, Sts. Irenaeus of Lyon and Clement of Alexandria, all base their interpretations of this text on an earlier Jewish tradition[13]. St. Athanasius in the fourth century rephrased the earlier assertion made by St. Irenaeus concerning Christ[14], which is now referred to as the "exchange formula": "He [Christ] became human that we might become divine." The passage from the second epistle of St. Peter (2 Pet. 1:4) was not often quoted until applied by St. Cyril of Alexandria to the Christological debates of the fifth century. In all these writings, it is said

---

11   *Ibid.,* 36.

12   *Ibid.,* 55-56. See also Hosea 1:10.

13   *Ibid.,* 56-57. In the early rabbinic tradition, the verses in Psalm 81 were originally addressed either to Adam and Eve at the time of their fall, or to the Israelites when they worshipped the golden calf in the desert after their exodus from Egypt.

14   *Ibid.,* 23-24.

that the divine nature that man shares is not the essential Being of God, but God's attributes of glory and goodness[15]. From the time of St. Irenaeus in the second century to St. Maximus the Confessor in the seventh century, the Church Fathers saw theosis as summarizing the very purpose of the Incarnation: the self-emptying love of God (*kenosis* in Greek) evoking a fervent human response (theosis), the result of which is the divinization of the human person mirroring the humanization of the divine Word[16].

The very intent of the Beatitudes is to issue the divine call for man to enter into the blessedness of the Divine Life via an eternal journey of the soul to blessed union with God. The very meaning of the Beatitudes is to illuminate the pathway to theosis by providing a step-by-step guide on how to advance to ever greater participation in the Divine Life.

In the preface to the Beatitudes (Matt. 5:1-2), Jesus went up the mountain for two reasons[17]. First, to fulfill the messianic prophecy of bringing the "good tidings" of the gospel (Luke 2:10-11; Isa. 40:9): "O You who bring good tidings to Zion, go into the high mountain; O You who bring good tidings to Jerusalem, lift up Your voice with strength; lift it up, be not afraid. Say to the cities of Judah, 'Behold your God'". Secondly, the proclamation of the "good tidings" from the "high mountain" is an invitation to all people to ascend the mountain with Him, to leave the low-ground of superficial and ignoble living, that one may reach the spiritual mountain of sublime contemplation[18].

---

15   *Ibid.,* 65. See 2 Pet. 1:3-7.

16   *Ibid.,* 39-40.

17   Anonymous, *Ancient Christian Commentary on Scripture: New Testament Ia; Matthew 1-13*, ed. Manlio Simonetti (Downers Grove, IL: InterVarsity Press, 2001), 78.

18   St. Gregory of Nyssa, *The Lord's Prayer, The Beatitudes*,

The divine word also says, "many Gentiles shall travel and say, 'Come and let us go up to the mountain of the Lord, to the house of the God of Jacob. He will proclaim His way to us, and we shall walk in it'" (Isa. 2:3), in order that God may be "beheld" by His people (cf. Isa. 40:9).

Furthermore, by ascending the mountain, Jesus showed by symbols and actions that He is the One who handed down the Mosaic Law on Mount Sinai (Exod. 19-20). At the same time, He is the One who is the author and the inaugurator of the New Covenant[19]. The blessings of the New Covenant are received by ascending the mountain. Moreover, the mountain is ascended by imitating Jesus Christ in what is possible for human nature – i.e., the dispositions and actions expressed in the Beatitudes – in order that the followers of Christ "may be partakers of the diving nature" through these "exceedingly great and precious promises" (2 Pet. 1:4; Isa. 2:3; 40:9), having put on the blessed form. The words of the Psalmist prefigure the blessedness of the good tidings of the divine call proclaimed by Christ in the Beatitudes when he says, "for there [the mountains of Zion] the Lord commanded the blessing and life forever" (Ps. 132:3).

Human nature is made to assimilate itself to the divine nature through *theognosis*[20] (cf. John 10:34-35;

85; Chrysostom, "Homily XV: Matt. V. 1,2", in *Nicene and Post-Nicene Fathers*, vol. 10, *Chrysostom: Homilies on the Gospel of Saint Matthew; First Series*, ed. Philip Schaff, 5th printing (Peabody, MA: Hendrickson, 2012), 91.

19 Chromatius, *Ancient Christian Commentary of Scripture: New Testament Ia: Matthew 1-13*, ed. Manlio Simonetti (Downers Grove, IL: InterVarsity Press, 2001), 78; Jer. 38:31-34; Matt. 26:28; 14:24; Luke. 22:17-19; John 6:53-58.

20 Vladimir Lossky, *Orthodox Theology: An Introduction*, trans. Ian and Ihita Kesarcodi-Watson (Crestwood, NY: St Vladimir's Press, 1978), 14-16, 18-20, 25; Vladimir Lossky, *The Mystical Theology of*

2 Pet. 1:2-4). Thus, the reality of theosis is possible for every person, provided the gifts of the image of God are cultivated (Mark. 4:1-9, 13-20). Consequently, theosis is achieved little-by-little through the step-by-step deification of human nature. This divine adoption is the calling and purpose of mankind[21]. However, human nature has been mortified in its state of separation from God through the Fall and individual sin (Rom. 3:23, 8:20). The good tidings of the gospel is that the potential to become like God was restored through the re-creation of humanity realized only by the Incarnation of Jesus Christ (2 Cor. 5:14-17). The redemptive work of the Incarnate Word once again opens the way for human beings to the achievement of theosis[22]. The Incarnate Christ brings us again to the Father and presents us with the potential of realizing the likeness of God (John 17:3, 9-11). The purpose of Christ's redemption of mankind is to restore the potential for theosis through union with the Holy Trinity (e.g., Gal. 4:4-7)[23]. Thus, there is an unending transformation into the likeness of God as man stretches beyond his nature to ever-greater

---

the Eastern Church (Crestwood, NY: St Vladimir's Press, [1957?]), 7-9. *Theognosis* is mystical knowledge of God, which starts from a fact: the revelation of God in Jesus Christ (Heb. 1:3; Col. 1:15), the beginning and ending points in theognosis (Heb. 12:2; Rev. 1:11; 22:13-14). It is a personal working out of the content of the common faith, which implies an existential encounter, reciprocity, with faith as a personal adherence to the personal presence of God who reveals Himself. It is communion: I know as I am known (cf. 1 Cor. 8:3). The initiative in theognosis belongs to God. The unknowable God reveals Himself. Because He transcends in His personal existence, in His very essence, He can really make Himself a participator in His divine economy (John 1:18).

21 Stavropoulos, *Partakers of Divine Nature*, 23-25.
22 *Ibid.*, 28-29.
23 Veniamin, *The Orthodox Understanding of Salvation*, 40.

participation in the Divine Life[24] through deifying grace (John 17:6-26; Eph. 1:3-6, 17-23; 2:22; 3:14-19; 4:11-13; I Pet. 1:3-4).

Theosis is objectively offered to us by the Incarnate, Crucified, Resurrected, Ascended God the Word. In Christ Jesus man finds his true place, "on the right hand of the Father" (cf. Mark 16:19; John 17:24), sharing in the Divine Life. In the same way that the two natures of Christ are united without confusion, man never ceases to be His creatures. God alone is Uncreated and Pre-eternal[25]. It is the Holy Spirit who subjectively transmits to humanity what is offered to us objectively by Christ (Gal. 4:6-7). Theosis, therefore, is achieved by uniting to our Lord Jesus Christ in baptism through in the Holy Spirit (Matt. 28:19-20; Mark 16:16; Acts 2:38-39; Rom 6:3-11; 8:1-17; Gal. 3:26-29; Col. 3:6-15), to the glory of God the Father (cf. 1 Pet. 1:1-2; Titus 3:4-7). Our human nature is restored and vivified by the Holy Spirit (John 3:5) through faith in Jesus Christ and by imitating His Life (John 3:14-16; 14:6), elevating us to knowledge of the Father (John 17:3) through the Mystery of the Church (Matt. 16:13-19; Eph. 2:19-22; 4:4-5, 11-16; 1 Cor. 12:12-14), which is communion with the Holy Trinity[26].

Theosis is once again within the reach of all who "put on Christ" (Gal. 3:27; 2 Cor. 5:17; Eph. 2:1-10). Assimilating to the likeness of God by becoming Christlike requires

---

24 Abraham J. Malherbe and Everett Ferguson, Introduction to *Gregory of Nyssa: The Life of Moses*, The Classics of Western Spirituality (New York: Paulist Press, 1978), 12.

25 Stavropoulos, *Partakers of Divine Nature.*, 40.

26 St. Basil the Great, *On the Holy Spirit*, ed. and intro. Stephen Hildebrand, Popular Patristic Series (Yonkers, NY: St Vladimir's Seminary Press, 2011), 83; John 14:6; 15:26; 16:3: 17:20-26; cf. Eph. 1:17-19

a purification of the passions, cultivation of the virtues, and living according to the commandments of Christ[27]. If we wish to be with Christ, we must become like Him (1 John 3:2-3). The Beatitudes are precise, *prophetic symbols*[28] of putting on Christ and becoming Christlike; thus, they reveal the pathway to theosis with respect to the personal, ascetic dimension of spiritual life. However, the context and background in which the Beatitudes are presented in the Gospel of St. Matthew are steeped in imagery and actions referring to the sacramental life of the Church. The ecclesial dimension of the Beatitudes and the spiritual life are discussed in detail in Chapter 2.

Theosis involves both the body and the soul (e.g., 1 Cor. 6:19; Rom. 12:1; 2 Cor. 3:18; 4:16-18). For this very reason, Jesus preceded His teachings on the Beatitudes by healing physical illnesses[29]. By healing the body from

---

27   Veniamin, *The Orthodox Understanding of Salvation*, 41.

28   Jerome Kodell, *The Eucharist in the New Testament*, Zacchaeus Studies: New Testament, General ed. Mary Ann Getty (Collegeville, MN: The Liturgical Press, 1988), 63. The word *symbol* is this book is understood by the concept of the Hebrew *prophetic symbol*. Nowadays, *symbol* is often understood in contradiction to something *real*. In the Hebrew mind, symbols were realities in their own right; the prophetic word made visible. The symbolic action in some sense brought the event into existence. This is the way the sacraments are understood. Thus, the concept of the Hebrew prophetic symbol was adopted by the Church and the Church Fathers. See also Norman Russell, *Fellow Workers with God: Orthodox Thinking on Theosis*, Book 5 of the Foundations Series (Crestwood, NY: St. Vladimir's Press, 2009), 98. St. Gregory Palamas spoke of *enhypostatic* symbols – i.e., something which is a symbol, but at the same time it is also that which is symbolizes. As a symbol, the Beatitudes are divine attributes knowable to sense and intellectual perception. As more than symbol, their imitation lead to inner transformation and participation in the Divine Life.

29   Chrysostom, "Homily XV: Matt. V. 1,2", in *Nicene and*

the base of the mountain (Matt. 4:23-25), signifying that the body is the lower part of human nature, Jesus showed by comparison that His teaching from the mountain top is for the mending of the soul, which is the higher part of human nature. Therefore, Jesus Christ is Maker of the whole creation (John 1:1-4). He cares for the entire person, and His healing ministry addresses physical and spiritual healing. Physical healing is woven together with spiritual healing and the forgiveness of sin[30]. Thus, teaching and instruction are mingled with the manifestation of the glory of Jesus Christ and His works[31], signifying that the Beatitudes proclaimed from the high mountain reveal the remedy for the healing of the soul and the body, which is the salvation and deification of man.

There are two possible ways to theognosis[32], both of which are expressed in the Beatitudes. One way is by cataphatic or positive theology, which proceeds by affirmations. The affirmations of cataphatic theology are the manifestations of the *energies*[33] of God in the economy.

Post-Nicene Fathers, 91.

30   Paul Meyendorff, *The Anointing of the Sick*, Book I of the Orthodox Liturgy Series (Crestwood, NY: St. Vladimir's Seminary Press, 2009), 78-80.

31   Chrysostom. "Homily XV: Matt. V. 1,2", in *Nicene and Post-Nicene Fathers*, 91.

32   Lossky, *The Mystical Theology of the Eastern Church*, 25. Here Lossky is summarizing the mystical theology of Pseudo-Dionysius the Areopagite, whose writings have been translated by Colm Luibheid, trans., Paul Rorem, forward, notes, and trans., Rene Roques, preface, Jaroslav Pelikan, Jean Leclercq, and Karlfried Froehlich, intro., *Pseudo-Dionysius: The Complete Works*, The Classics of Western Spirituality (Mahwah, NY: Paulist Press, 1987).

33   Metropolitan Hilarion Alfeyev, *Orthodox Christianity Volume II: Doctrine and Teaching of the Orthodox Church*, trans. Andrew Smith (Yonkers, NY: St. Vladimir's Press, 2012), 153-154. The term

Stated another way, positive theology comes down to us in a "ladder of theophanies", so to speak, in which God condescends toward us in the revelation of His energies[34]. A succinct description of the ladder of theophanies is the seven-fold operation of the Holy Spirit (Isa. 11:2-3), the order of which proceeds from the more excellent degrees of God's energies to lesser degrees: wisdom, understanding, counsel, might, knowledge, godliness, and the fear of God[35]. The seven-fold operation of the Spirit is incarnated by our Lord and God and Savior Jesus Christ (Isa. 11:1; Matt. 3:16). Therefore, by imitating Christ, the soul participates in these energies of God, leading to inner sanctification by the deifying grace of the Holy Spirit, and the elevation of the soul to the knowledge of the Father (cf. 1 Pet. 1:1-2; Titus 3:4-7), which having put on this blessed form, is advancement toward theosis.

The purpose of cataphatic theognosis is to reveal the energies of God in the descending ladder of theophanies

---

energy (*Greek energiai*) in Orthodox Theology connotes "activities." St. Gregory Palamas showed that the divine energies of God are the connecting link between God and the created world, not as a "mediator" but containing God Himself, who extends outside His essence. Thus, the energies or "activities" of God differ from the essence of God. Essence and energies provide a terminology to discuss the paradox that God is invisible in His essence (e.g., Exo. 33:20). At the same time, God reveals Himself to those deemed worthy (e.g., Gen. 32:30; Exod. 33:11; Deut. 34:10; I John 3:2). St. Basil the Great described it this way: "we know our God by His energies, but we do not pretend that we can draw near to His essence; for His energies descend to us, but His essence remains inaccessible."

34   Lossky, *The Mystical Theology of the Eastern Church*, 39-40.

35   Augustin, "Our Lord's Sermon on the Mount: Book I", in *Nicene and Post-Nicene Fathers*, vol. 6, *Augustin: Sermon on the Mount, Harmony of the Gospels, Homilies on the Gospels*; *First Series*, ed. Philip Schaff, 5th printing (Peabody, MA: Hendrickson Publishers, 2012), 6.

in order that the soul may ascend these very same steps. The ascent of the ladder of theophanies is the other way of theognosis: apophatic or negative theology, which proceeds by negations. Apophatic theology is an approach that extends beyond affirmative knowledge of God towards mystical union with God, with God's nature simultaneously remaining inaccessible and incomprehensible[36], an approach to theognosis that is appropriate with respect to the radical transcendence of God[37]. Every word, term, attribute, and concept are a part of human language and thought, suited for the created order, but cannot contain the reality of the Uncreated Divine Being[38]. The perfection of apophaticism is the dissolution of subject and object in contemplation. In other words, God no longer presents Himself as object. In this perfected state of man, which is deification or salvation, theognosis is no longer affirmative knowledge of God but the experience of communion with the Divine Hypostases[39] of the Holy Trinity.

The way of apophatic theology is to ascend the steps of the ladder of theophanies from lesser degrees of the energies of God to the more excellent degrees, and to extend beyond these theophanies towards union with God. Therefore, apophatic theology presupposes a series of genuine contemplation and inward purification (John 17:3; 1 Thess. 4:7-8). To contemplate God is to assimilate

---

36 Lossky, *The Mystical Theology of the Eastern Church*, 28.

37 Lossky, *Orthodox Theology: An Introduction*, 23-25.

38 Metropolitan Hilarion, *Orthodox Christianity Volume II*, 158.

39 Vladimir Lossky, *Dogmatic Theology: Creation, God's Image in Man, & the Redeeming Work of the Holy Trinity*, A Revised, Annotated, and Expanded Second Edition of *Theologie dogmatique*, ed. Olivier Clement and Michel Stavrou, trans. Anthony P. Gythiel (Yonkers, NY: Saint Vladimir's Press, 2017), 191. This term is used to describe the three Persons of the Holy Trinity. It is a Greek term for person.

to the likeness of God revealed in the theophanies, which is inextricably linked to inner purification (1 Pet. 1:15-16). By progressing in the series of contemplation and inner purification in the ascension of the ladder of theophanies, intellectual knowledge gives way to experience. This experience of faith through the ontological relationship between God and man transforms the soul into union with God through deifying grace[40] (John 17:6-26).

The Beatitudes are given by the prophetic teaching of Jesus Christ in the order of the lesser degrees of the energies of God to the more excellent degrees, which correspond to the seven-fold operation of the Holy Spirit, but with the order reversed[41]. For example, "poor in spirit" (Matt. 5:3), or humility, corresponds to "the fear of God" (Isa. 11:3), and so on, with "peacemaker" (Matt. 5:9) corresponding to "wisdom" (Isa. 11:2). This correspondence between the seven-fold operation of the Holy Spirit and the first seven Beatitudes will be expounded in subsequent chapters. The content of the Beatitudes, which is the seven-fold operation

---

40   Lossky, *Orthodox Theology: An Introduction*, 16. There is an internally objective relationship for which the catechumen prepares. Stated simply, that relationship is to become adopted sons of the Father through Jesus Christ, our Brother, in the Holy Spirt Who is our Helper and Comforter (Eph. 1:3-6, 13-14; Heb. 2:10-13; John 14:16; 16:7). It is through the sacraments of Baptism and Chrismation that the ontological participation in the Holy Trinity is conferred upon the faithful (Gal. 3:27; Ro. 6:3-11; John 3:5; 16:14-15). Through the gift of Christ in Baptism (Gal. 3:27; Ro. 6:3-11), we have been restored to our true nature; thus, we have been recreated in the image of God (2 Cor. 5:17). Moreover, through the gift of the Holy Spirit in Chrismation, our new nature is vivified (Acts 1:8; 2:17-21), opening to us the way to deification or union with God through the progressive assimilation to the likeness of God (2 Pet. 1:2-11).

41   Augustin, "Our Lord's Sermon on the Mount: Book I", in *Nicene and Post-Nicene Fathers*, 6.

of the Holy Spirit (Isa. 11:2-3) incarnated through the life and ministry of Jesus Christ (Isa. 61:1-6), combined with the order in which they were presented by Jesus, reflects the two-fold, complementary ways of theognosis.

Therefore, the good tidings of the gospel, the fulfillment of the prophetic word, is the illumination of the pathway to theosis expressed by the Beatitudes (cf. Ps. 118:105, 123). To "walk" in the pathway to theosis is to ascend the ladder of theophanies revealed in the Beatitudes. The ladder of theophanies are the revelation of the Father through the Only-Begotten Son in the Holy Spirit (John 3:16; 14:6; 16:12-15; Heb. 1:1-4). The ladder of Beatitudes is ascended when the follower of Christ incarnates the virtues expressed by the Beatitude by imitating the Incarnate Word in everyday life. The ascension is achieved by progressively setting aside all that can be affirmed about God[42]. At each step in the ascent to union with God, the concepts, images, and ideas disclosed by each Beatitude are cast aside, in the sense that they shackle and imprison the spirit within human thought. The mystical aspect of theognosis is that instead of assimilating the divine mystery – i.e., the data of revelation – to human modes of understanding, a profound inner transformation takes place in the faithful (Ro. 6:4-5; 1 Thess. 4:7; 2 Pet. 1:3-4). The apophatic attitude opens up boundless horizons for contemplation and inner sanctification at each step in the ascent of the virtues revealed in the Beatitudes toward union with God (e.g., 2 Cor. 5:17; 2 Pet. 1:5-8), according to the capacity of the soul and the degree to which it has assimilated to the virtue exemplified by each Beatitude.

In His teaching from the high mountain, Jesus proclaimed traditional apocalyptic beatitudes[43] (Matt.

---

42   Lossky, *The Mystical Theology of the Eastern Church*, 25.

43   Dennis Hamm, *The Beatitudes in Context: What Luke and Matthew Meant*, ed. Mary Ann Getty, Zacchaeus Studies: New Testament

5:3-10). But in the context of His preaching of the kingdom of God and His healing ministry (Matt. 4:17, 23-25), these beatitudes outstripped their traditional function of exhortation[44]. The expected Reign of God is now accessible. This possibility is made explicit within the Beatitudes themselves: "Blessed are the poor in spirit, for theirs is the kingdom of heaven ... Blessed are those who are persecuted for righteousness sake, for theirs is the kingdom of heaven" (Matt. 5:3, 10). As theological language, the Beatitudes incorporate a projection of eschatology into the present. The purpose of theological language is not to imprison the mind to human conceptions of the divine nature, but to open the mind to a reality which goes beyond it[45].

(Wilmington, Delaware: Michael Glaziar, 1990), 7-9. The modern technical term used to describe the literary form of beatitudes found in the Scriptures is *macarism*. There are two forms of OT macarisms: wisdom beatitudes (e.g., Ps. 1; 111; 126:5; 127:1-6; 143:12-15; and Ecclus. 25:7-11) and apocalyptical beatitudes (e.g., Dan. 12:12-13, 14). Most of the NT macarisms are apocalyptical beatitudes (e.g., James 1:12). The English word beatitude comes from the Latin adjective beatus, which means "fortunate". The Greek adjective form of the plural noun that begins each of the classical beatitudes is makariori, which means "fortunate", "happy", or "blessed". Makariori and beatus are translations of the Hebrew adjective ashre, which means "fortunate" or "blessed". The usage of ashre in the Hebrew Bible is never to describe a subjective emotional state, but rather a situation deriving from one's relationship to God. Therefore, the adjective ashre is better translated "blessed" rather than "happy" or "fortunate." The Greek word makarios (singular), or makariori (pluaral), was a suitable word to translate the Hebrew word ashre. In Hellenistic Greek, makarios already had divine associations. Homer called the Greek gods makariori. By extension, humans were called makariori when they were thought of as participating in the happiness of the gods.

44 *Ibid.*, 24-25.
45 Lossky, *Orthodox Theology: An Introduction*, 13-15.

Even within the literary form of the Beatitudes, given the context from which they were proclaimed, their teachings illuminate a pathway to ever-greater participation in the Divine Life through a step-by-step assimilation to the likeness of God.

The Evangelists and the Church Fathers recognized the Beatitudes as an ascent of the ladder of theophanies leading to theosis. Specifically, the order and content of the Gospel of St. Matthew in chapters 3-7 reflect this recognition. The setting of Jesus's preaching of the Beatitudes from the high mountain recorded by St. Matthew acknowledges this event as a fulfillment of messianic prophecy (e.g., Isa. 2:3; 40:9), as discussed above. Furthermore, the macarism form of the Beatitudes, combined with His healing and preaching ministries, reveal that the kingdom of God is now accessible through Jesus Christ (Matt. 4:17, 23-25; 7:26-27). Christ is inaugurating the New Covenant (Jer. 38:31-34; 39:39-41; 40:6; 2 Cor. 3:2-3; Heb. 10:15-18), which, in short, is "the kingdom of God is within you" (Luke 17:21; see also Ez. 36:26-27). The potential for this mystical union between the followers of Christ and God is the inauguration of a new condition of human nature, brought about through the Incarnation by the *hypostatic* and (dynamic) *energetic* union of the divine and human natures of the One Christ[46]. The energetic aspect of the union of the divine and human natures of Christ forms the basis of

---

46 Veniamin, *The Orthodox Understanding of Salvation*, 16-18. The *hypostatic* union is an *essential* union. Christ is a divine Person, the Person of the Word of God, the Only-Begotten Son of God, and the Person of the Son of Man. But the union of the divine and human natures of Christ is also energetic: there is an interpenetration of the natural energy of each of the two natures of Christ. The theological term for the energetic union of the divine and human natures in Christ is called *communicatio idiomatum*.

the Christian's participation in the Divine Life[47], and is also the mode by which the imitator of Christ achieves theosis (Matt. 5:48; John 14:6; Eph. 5:1-2). As a finite, created being, participation in the Divine Life for the follower of Christ implies both the gift of God concomitant with a personal striving and perpetual journey of progress in the virtuous life[48]. As the Psalmist said, "Blessed is the man whose help is from You, O Lord; He purposed ascents in his heart in the valley of weeping, into the place he appointed; For there the lawgiver shall give blessings. They shall go from strength to strength; The God of gods shall be seen in Zion" (Ps. 83:6-7).

Progress toward mystical union with God, through the apophatic approach of assimilating the Beatitudes, is achieved through a series of inner transformation brought about by contemplation and inner purification. According to St. Gregory of Nyssa, there are three stages in the ascent of the soul to God[49]. Inner purification is the first stage, which is the struggle to overcome the passions and to develop the virtues, the *praxis* (literally "action") to purify the heart, constituting genuine repentance[50]. Praxis naturally leads to contemplation, the second stage, which is the vision of the glory of God. The third stage follows contemplation and illumination, which is participation in the Divine Life. These are preparatory stages leading to theosis, gradually stretching and extending the person

---

47 Russell, *Fellow Workers with God: Orthodox Thinking on Theosis*, 127.

48 Lossky, *The Mystical Theology of the Eastern Church*, 28.

49 Russell, *Fellow Workers with God: Orthodox Thinking on Theosis*, 130.

50 Hierotheos, Metropolitan of Nafpaktos, *The Illness and Cure of the Soul in the Orthodox Tradition*, Rev. 2nd ed., trans. Effie Mavromichali (Lavadia Greece: Birth of the Theotokos Monastery, 2010), 36.

beyond his nature through the apophatic approach and disposition. However, these stages themselves do not constitute theosis. Through *synergy*[51] between human *ascetic*[52] efforts and deifying grace (Eph. 5:1; Phil. 2:12-13), ascending through these preparatory stages, man acquires something he did not possess by nature, which is union with God (John 10:34-35; Ps. 81:6; Eph. 1:3-6; 2 Cor. 8:9; 2 Pet. 1:3-4).

The characteristics and goal of the apophatic stages discussed above were foreshadowed and prefigured in the Israelite's escape from Egypt and Moses's ascent of Mount Sinai. The ascent of Moses recorded in the Book of Exodus has always been associated with the ascent to mystical knowledge of God and union with Him[53]. Moreover, the

---

51   Timothy Ware (Bishop Kallistos of Diokleia), *The Orthodox Church*, New Edition (London: Penguin Book, 1997), 221-222. The term *synergy* (*synergeia* in Greek) means co-operation. It is the word the Church Fathers used to describe the relationship between divine grace and human freedom. The origin of the usage of this term is traced to the words of the Apostle Paul: "For we are God's fellow workers (*synergoi*)" (1 Cor. 3:9). See also Russell, *Fellow Workers with God: Orthodox Thinking on Theosis*, 149. Synergism implies that human energy necessarily participates in salvation – i.e., in the assimilation of deification, even if this participation is diminished by original sin.

52   Veniamin, *The Orthodox Understanding of Salvation*, 31. *Asceticism* comes from the Greek word *ascesis*. The meaning is understood as "spiritual labors". The necessity of personal asceticism for growth in the grace of God toward theosis reflects the spirit of Holy Scripture. See Lewis J. Patsavos, *Spiritual Dimensions of the Holy Canons* (Brookline, MA: Holy Cross Orthodox Press, 2003) 54-55. All must through ascesis become "violent" ("viastai", Matt. 11:12) – i.e., violence must be employed in subjugating the rebellious, sinful nature to do the holy will of God. From this perspective, every genuine Christian must be an ascetic.

53   Vladimir Lossky, *In the Image and Likeness of God*, ed. John H.

Evangelist's arrangement of the structure and content of chapter 3-7 of the Gospel of Matthew show that Christ is the "Way" to the Uncreated Existing One (Exod. 3:14; John 1:18; 14:6), the fulfillment and perfection of Moses's ascent to God, with the Beatitudes illuminating the pathway to theosis. Thus, the focus of the next chapter is an exegesis and typological analysis of this significant episode in God's economy of salvation, which provides essential preparation for the Beatitudes revealed by Jesus Christ in His Sermon on the Mount.

> But I press on, that I may lay hold of that for which Christ Jesus also laid hold of me. (Phil. 3:12)

Erickson and Thomas E. Bird, intro. John Meyendorff (Crestwood, NY: St Vladimir's Press, 1974), 32-40.

Chapter 2:
The Ascent of Moses on Mount Sinai

Again the Lord said to Moses, "Go down and solemnly charge the people and sanctify them today and tomorrow, and let them wash their closes. Let them be ready for the third day, for on the third day the Lord will descend upon Mount Sinai in the sight of all the people. You shall set bounds for the people all around, saying 'Take heed to yourselves that you do not go up to the mountain or touch its base. Whoever touches the mountain will surely die..." Now all the people witnessed the thunderings, the lightning flashes, the sound of the trumpet, and the mountain smoking; and when the people saw this, they trembled and stood afar off... So the people stood afar off, but Moses drew near the thick darkness where God was. (Ex. 19:10-12; 20:18, 21)

The spiritual meaning of the events accompanying the ascent of Moses on Mount Sinai is a foreshadow of the content and the events associated with the preaching and teaching of the Beatitudes by Jesus Christ at the Sermon on the Mount (cf. Isa. 2:3; 40:9). Moses's ascent is a typology of the journey of the soul to God through the eternal development of the virtues expressed by the Beatitudes (cf. Titus 2:11-14; 3:3-7; 1 Cor. 10:1-11; 2 Cor. 3:7-18), leading to the experience of communion with God (Matt. 5:3, 10). The ascent of Moses on Mount Sinai illustrates the superiority of mystical knowledge of God compared to sense perception and intellectual knowledge[54]. Moreover, the ascent of Moses is a paradigm of the necessity in theognosis of progress in the virtuous life through a series of contemplation and inner purification[55].

Achievements in the spiritual life, however, do not occur in a vacuum. They are personal and communal rather than individual (e.g., Eph. 2:19-22; 4:1-6, 11-16). Hence, spiritual transformation emerges from the context of a life of repentance and participation in the sacramental life of the Church, through synergy of the grace of God and the ascetic struggle of the person to overcome the passions and to develop the virtues (e.g., Eph. 4:17-32; 5:1-21). This is also revealed typologically by the events recorded in the Book of Exodus pertaining to the Israelites' escape from Egypt and their experiences in the desert leading up to Moses's ascent of Mount Sinai.

The events of the Book of Exodus and the figure of Moses have always occupied a prominent place in the writings of both Jews and Christians concerning the knowledge of God[56]. Building upon the exegetical traditions of Philo, the Hellenized Jew from Alexandria, and the Church Fathers from the Alexandrian school, St. Gregory of Nyssa developed a comprehensive typological interpretation of the Book of Exodus in his writings on *The Life of Moses*[57]. This work provides an essential foundation

---

54 Lossky, *In the Image and Likeness of God*, 13-14.

55 *Ibid.*, 32-33.

56 *Ibid.*, 32-40.

57 Abraham J. Malherbe and Everett Ferguson, Introduction to

for reaping the full harvest of spiritual fruit from the Beatitudes of Jesus Christ, a work which also forms the fundamental basis of the typological interpretation and theological conclusions developed in this chapter.

The Crossing of the Red Sea (Exod. 14) prefigures the mystical waters of baptism[58]. Those who pass through the

---

Gregory of Nyssa: The Life of Moses, 5-9, 12-13. The format of St. Gregory's *Life of Moses* is based on the work of Philo of Alexandria, who also wrote a two-part *Life of Moses*: the *historia*, which summarizes the historical events of Moses's life from the biblical accounts in the Books of Exodus and Numbers, followed by the *theoria*, which are spiritual lessons derived from the historical events. St. Gregory also uses the allegorical method of Philo as the basis for a biblical interpretation of the OT. The Alexandrian school absorbed, appropriated, and transformed the allegorical method of Philo in the elucidation of Christian doctrine. St. Clement of Alexandria shows the first extensive use of Philo's allegorical method. However, Origen of Alexandria is the closest in method and content to St. Gregory's interpretation of the OT. Nevertheless, Gregory goes beyond Origen. For Origen, the spiritual interpretation of the OT is an interiorization of the sacraments. On the other hand, Gregory takes the moral allegories of Philo and extends them in the direction of mystical union with God, in his application of the allegorical method to the interpretation to the spiritual life. St. Gregory belongs to the Alexandrian school of interpretation, but his nonliteral interpretations also incorporate certain common Christian interpretations of the OT, especially with reference to Christ, the Church, and Christian ordinances. While the material and method of his interpretation are old, St. Gregory's synthesis is new and original. The goal of the spiritual life in the Platonic-based system of Origen is a static unity with God. The modification that St. Gregory made to Alexandrian spirituality is that the goal of the spiritual life dynamic, an eternal progress toward mystical union with God, which is the mark of perfection.

58   Gregory of Nyssa, *The Life of Moses*, trans. and intro. Everett Ferguson and Abraham J. Malherbe, preface by John Meyendorff, The Classics of Western Spirituality (Mahwah, New Yrok: Paulist Press, 1978), 83-84 (II, 125-127; this numbering scheme refers to

saving waters must put to death all manner of evil. Nothing from the old life should emerge from the waters, indicating a complete break with the continuity of evil. The death of the first born (Exod. 12:29-36) lays down the principle that it is impossible to flee the Egyptian life without destroying utterly the first born of evil[59]. A new beginning in life is the work of both God and man (Exod. 12:21-28; Rom. 6:3-11; Col. 2:11-15; 3:1-17). Only God can make the waters of baptism effectual for a new beginning (Exod. 14:13-14, 26-31; Titus 3:4-7). But man must cooperate with God by emerging from the waters alone, not dragging along the Egyptian army of evil with him (Titus 2:11-14).

There are two guides in the new life for those who progress in virtue: Moses, who represents the Law, and the "cloud", which represents a proper understanding of the Law[60]. Moses prefigures Christ (Heb. 3:1-6; 9:11-22), who is the Lawgiver (John 5:46; 8:58) and the one who fulfilled the Law (Matt. 5:17-18). The cloud prefigures the grace of the Holy Spirit[61] (cf. Matt. 24:29-31; 2 Thess. 2:13-17), who will sanctify (1 Pet. 1:1-2) and "guide you into all truth" (John 16:13). This historical episode in the exodus of the Israelites from Egypt foreshadows the Church's Sacraments of Baptism and Chrismation.

Life removed from the passions and the Egyptian pleasures of evil seem difficult and unpleasant at the beginning of the virtuous life. This is the spiritual meaning of the bitter waters of Marah, which were made sweet by placing the wood into the waters (Exod. 15:22-26). The

---

the book number (II) and paragraph/section number (125-127) of the original manuscript. This numbering scheme will be given in parenthesis for all subsequent reference to this work).

59 *Ibid.*, 75 (II, 90).

60 *Ibid.*, 92 (II, 153).

61 *Ibid.*, 82-83 (II, 121).

wood prefigures the Cross of Jesus Christ[62]. Thus, the difficult struggle in acquiring virtue is made sweet by the hope of the resurrection (2 Pet. 1:3).

The Israelites were refreshed when they camped at Elim, "where there were twelve fountains of water and seventy palm trees" (Exod. 15:27). The springs foreshadow the Twelve Apostles[63], whom the Lord chose for His service, and through whom He caused His word to spring forth (cf. Ps. 67:27). The seventy palms represent apostles appointed by Jesus in addition to the Twelve (e.g., Luke 10:1-24). Therefore, those who rest in the Gospel teachings find refreshment for the journey to God (cf. Ps. 17:21-25, 36; 1 John 5:2-4).

The true food to nourish the soul in its journey to God is manna, the bread from heaven (Exod. 16:4-5, 14-16). This prefigures the mystery of the Sacrament of the Eucharist (John 6:58). The heavenly bread is not incorporeal[64]. It is the Word made flesh (John 1:14). "Then Jesus said to them, 'Most assuredly I say to you, unless you eat the flesh of the Son of Man and drink His blood, you have no life in you.... This is the bread which came down from heaven – not as your fathers ate the manna and are dead. He who eats this bread will live forever'" (John 6:53, 58).

Jesus Christ is also the "spiritual Rock" and the "living stone" (1 Cor. 10:4; 1 Pet. 2:4; cf. Exod. 17:5-7). To the disobedient and unbelieving, Jesus is "a stone of stumbling and a rock of offense" (Isa. 28:16; cf. 1 Pet. 2:7-8; Exod. 17:7). By employing the rod of faith (Exod. 17:5-6), on the other hand, Christ the living stone becomes drink to those who are thirsty and abides in those who receive Him

---

62   *Ibid.*, 85-86 (II, 131-132).

63   *Ibid.*, 86 (II, 134).

64   *Ibid.*, 88 (II, 139-140).

(John 6:56). Jesus also said, "but the water I shall give him will become in him a fountain of water springing up into eternal life" (John 4:14).

Progress in the journey to God requires synergy of unequal but equally necessary movements[65]: divine grace and the cooperation of human will and action (e.g., 1 Cor. 3:9). The historical events recounted above reveal the divine gifts of God for the salvation, protection, and preservation of His people, which find their ultimate fulfillment in the Sacraments of the Church. To reap the fruits of these gifts, however, man must mingle with them his ascetic effort to overcome the enemy of sin and to develop the virtues. This is the spiritual meaning of the Israelite's war with Amalek[66]. As the Psalmist said, "It is God ... Who teaches my hands to make war; and You make my arms a bronze bow; and You gave me the shield of Your salvation; and Your right hand supported me ... For You armed me with strength for war; You entangled under my feet all who rose up against me, and You gave me the back of my enemies; and You destroyed all who hate me" (Ps. 17:35-36, 40-41).

The one who is nourished by the Sacraments of the Church, and who delights in the Gospel teachings, is ready to do battle with sin and the passions, a battle that is as inevitable for Christians as it was for the Israelites (Exod. 17:8-16; Eph. 6:10-13; 2 Cor. 10:3-6). The battle is waged under the leadership of Joshua, the general of Israel who has traditionally been regarded as a type of Jesus[67]. Moreover, the Israelites gained victory over the enemy when Moses

---

65 Timothy Ware (Bishop Kallistos of Diokleia), *The Orthodox Church*, New Edition (London: Penguin Books, 1997), 221-222.

66 Gregory of Nyssa, *The Life of Moses*, 90-91 (II, 147-151).

67 *Ibid.*, 174 (footnote 169). In Greek, the names Joshua and Jesus are identical. Philo, the Hellenized Jew from Alexandria, already discerned that 'Joshua' should be interpreted as 'salvation.'

held up his hands (Exod. 17:11), forming the shape of a cross with his body. Thus, the cause and monument of victory over sin is the Cross of Jesus Christ, to those who look to it with the rod of faith (Exod. 17:9). As the Scripture says, "there is no other name [than Jesus, a name identical to Joshua in Greek] under heaven given among men by which we must be saved" (Acts 4:12).

The preceding teachings emphasize the advancements that one must accomplish before approaching the mountain of divine knowledge[68]. The pathway to union with God is foreshadowed by Moses's ascent of Mount Sinai, by the thundering sound of the trumpets from the mountain, and the entry of Moses at the apex of the mountain into the darkness where God is (Exod. 19:1-25; 20:18-21). The Psalmist also interprets Moses's ascent of Mount Sinai as a typology of union with God: "Who shall ascend to the mountain of the Lord? Who shall stand is His holy place? He who has innocent hands and a pure heart; He who does not lift up his soul in vain; He who does not swear deceitfully to his neighbor. He shall receive blessing from the Lord and mercy from the God of his salvation" (Ps. 23:3-5). Blessed is the one who has reached the heights of participation in the Divine Life through inner purification and contemplation.

St. Matthew the Evangelist also understood the universal and salvific meaning of the Israelite's flight from Egypt leading up to Moses's ascent of Mount Sinai. The content and arrangement of chapters 3-7 of the Gospel of Matthew conform to this episode in God's economy. The climax of this section of Matthew's Gospel is the Beatitudes, which reveal the pathway to theosis as the universal and salvific fulfillment of Moses's ascent of Mount Sinai.

---

68   *Ibid.*, 91-92 (II, 152).

Religious knowledge comes initially to those who receive it as the light of God[69] (John 8:12). The Decalogue, therefore, was the product of divine illumination received by Moses from God at the summit of Mount Sinai. The Decalogue reflects the two sides of religious virtue[70]. On one side, virtue pertains to a proper religious knowledge of the Divine. This side is reflected in the first tablet of the Decalogue, which pertains to love for God (cf. Matt. 22:37-38). Moses had come to know that the Divine is beyond all knowledge and understanding: "Moses drew near the thick darkness where God was" (Exod. 20:21), for "He [God] made darkness His hiding place" (Ps. 17:12). The other side of religious virtue is right conduct, or the purity of life. This side is reflected in the second tablet of the Decalogue, which is related to love for neighbor (Matt. 22:39-40).

The Beatitudes also reflect these two sides of virtue, but with the added divine promise of union with God to all those who approach and ascend the divine mountain through Christ (e.g., Isa. 2:3; 40:9; Heb. 12:18-24). Just as Moses provided additional commentary and expository teaching on the meaning of the Decalogue following its issuance from Mount Sinai, as recorded in the Books of Exodus and Deuteronomy, Jesus unpacked the meaning of the Beatitudes in the remainder of the Sermon on the Mount, which is essentially the deeper spiritual meaning of the Decalogue, leading to theosis through deifying grace.

St. John the Forerunner "came preaching in the wilderness of Judaea, and saying, 'Repent, for the kingdom of heaven is at hand!'" (Matt. 3:1-2). St. John's ministry anchors the Gospel of Jesus Christ to the episode in Israel's history when they were encamped in the desert before the

---

69   *Ibid.*, 94-95 (II, 162-163).

70   *Ibid.*, 96 (II, 166).

holy mountain of Sinai, just prior to Moses's ascent (Exod. 19:1-2). The desert origin of the Forerunner's ministry, his message of repentance and his work of baptizing the penitents in the Jordon, along with his own ascetic lifestyle, communicate very powerfully that the prophet symbols, to which the historical events of Israel's exodus from Egypt point, are about to obtain their ultimate fulfillment. The authenticity of this correlation between the events recorded in the Book of Exodus and the ministry of St. John the Forerunner comes from the prophetic word of Scripture and their interpretation by the divine Word: "For this is he [John the Baptist] of whom it is written: 'Behold, I send My messenger before Your face, Who will prepare Your way before You.' Assuredly, I say to you, among those born of women there has not risen one greater than John the Baptist" (Matt. 11:10-11; cf. Matt. 3:1-6). The Forerunner is leading the people to the holy mountain, a path which can only be traveled by way of repentance. He is preparing the way for communion with God through The Christ, by ascending the holy mountain with Christ, to all who heed the divine call.

Just as the Israelites had to achieve certain progress in the life of virtue before approaching the mountain of divine knowledge, St. John the Forerunner also taught that preparation through repentance and development of spiritual fruit are prerequisites of theognosis: "Therefore, bear fruits worthy of repentance" (Matt. 3:8). Moreover, the Forerunner taught that the children of Abraham are not defined in terms of a genetic link (cf. Matt. 3:9), thereby extending the blessing of Abraham and his offspring beyond ethnic Jews (Rom. 4:5-12). Abraham attained friendship with God by actualizing the divine gift of election through faith and the working out of the content of his faith (cf. James 2:23; Heb. 11:8-17).

All aspects of the Forerunner's ministry – his desert origin, his ascetic witness, and his words and actions – have their root in Israel's exodus from Egypt and the preparatory stages leading to the mountain of divine knowledge. However, St. John makes clear that the salvific content contained in these prophetic symbols will be brought to fruition and realized by The Christ. "I indeed baptize you with water unto repentance, but He who is coming after me is mightier than I, whose sandals I am not worthy to carry. He will baptize you with the Holy Spirit and fire" (Matt. 3:11).

Moses's ascent of Mount Sinai teaches the way to knowledge of the transcendent God[71]. The sacraments of initiation (Baptism, Chrismation, and the Eucharist), the continual nourishment from the Sacrament of the Eucharist, catechetical teaching and the beginning of the acquisition of virtue, as represented by the historical episodes discussed above in Israel's exodus from Egypt, are preconditions that must be attained before approaching the base of the mountain, the ascent of which leads to union with God.

The mountain of divine knowledge is steep and difficult to climb[72]. The multitude are not capable of the ascent (Exod. 19:21-24; cf. Matt. 5:1), although all possess the potentiality for the ascent through the divine call and the gift of the image of God. As Jesus said, the way to participation in the Divine Life is "by the narrow gate" (Matt. 7:13). Once the beginning of the virtuous life takes root through the preparatory stages, progress in theognosis is achieved through contemplation and continual purity of body and soul[73]. This is revealed by God when he instructed

---

71   *Ibid.*, 92 (II, 153-154).

72   *Ibid.*, 93 (II, 158).

73   *Ibid.*, 92-93 (II, 154-156).

Moses to solemnly charge the people at the base of the mountain to sanctify themselves and wash their garments (Exod. 19:10, 14-15). Washing the clothes refers to purifying the outer garments of the flesh and the outward pursuits of life[74]. Sanctifying oneself refers to the inner purification of the soul.

Theognosis is acquired through continual progress in the life of virtue, which demands asceticism[75]. The passions must be controlled. This principle was established emphatically with the death of the first born (Exod. 12:29-36), as discussed previously, and now by God's command that the people sanctify themselves and wash their garments at the base of the mountain (Exod. 19:10, 14-15). In addition, the animals were not allowed to touch the base of the mountain and live (Exod. 19:13). Irrational animals are governed by sensual appetites[76]. The Apostle Paul notes that sensual knowledge also includes the perception of the mind (1 Cor. 2:9). Thus, the ascetic struggle in the development of virtue includes keeping the sensual appetites and intellectual perceptions under control and keeping the body and soul stainless[77].

The sound of the trumpet blast from Mount Sinai represents the Prophets and the Apostles[78]. The imagery of a trumpet blast can be discerned from the Psalmist's description of the pronouncement of the gospel message to the world: "Their proclamation went forth into all the earth, and their words to the ends of the world" (Ps. 18:5).

---

74 *Ibid.*, 92-93 (II, 154-155).

75 *Ibid.*, 55 (II, 2).

76 *Ibid.*, 93 (II, 156).

77 Abraham J. Malherbe and Everett Ferguson, Introduction to *Gregory of Nyssa: The Life of Moses*, 10.

78 Gregory of Nyssa, *The Life of Moses*, 93-94 (II, 159).

The Apostles and Prophets, as instruments of God (2 Tim. 3:16-17), trumpeted the divine mystery of the Incarnation[79]. As Moses advanced up the mountain, the sound of the trumpet became longer and louder until its sound became intelligible, and Moses conversed with God (Exod. 19:19). But the multitude at the base of mountain were not capable of hearing the voice from above (Exod. 19:16; 20:18-19). They relied on Moses to teach them divine truth, which he heard from on high as he ascended to greater heights.

As Moses continued to ascend the mountain, he surpassed all visible manifestations of God – the thundering and lightning, the smoke and fire, the trumpet blast, and even the intelligible voice of God (Exod. 19:16-19). The climax of Moses's ascent is when, at the invocation of God (Exod. 19:20, 24), he "drew near the thick darkness where God was" (Exod. 20:21). The notion of the Divine seen in darkness seems contradictory at first, since the first theophany seen by Moses was in the light of the burning bush (Exod. 3:2). Moreover, St. John the Evangelist said, "God is light and in Him is no darkness at all" (1 John 1:5). That God was seen by Moses in the darkness represents the ultimate inaccessibility and incomprehensibility of God, as understood by Jewish tradition, through the writings of Philo, and by the Church Fathers[80]. According the Pseudo-Dionysius the Areopagite, God is light in the sense that He manifests Himself and can be contemplated in His energies. Divine darkness in the inaccessible light (1 Tim. 6:16). In other words, God by His nature remains transcendent, even in the immanence of His manifestation[81]. In advancing

---

79   *Ibid.*, 93-94 (II, 158-159).

80   Lossky, *In the Image and Likeness of God*, 13-14, 32-40; Lossky, *The Mystical Theology of the Eastern Church*, 25-27.

81   Loosky, *In the Image and Likeness of God*, 39-40.

through the series of contemplation in ascending the mountain of divine knowledge, Moses came to see that the divine nature is uncontemplated. Knowledge of the divine essence is unattainable not only by men but by every intelligent creature (1 John 1:18).

In approaching union with God, one must leave behind everything that is observed[82]: what the bodily senses comprehend and what the intelligence thinks it sees. This is reflected in the first three commandments of the Decalogue proclaimed by the divine word (Exod. 20:2-3), affirming what Moses had learned in the darkness[83]. The Lord forbade the Divine to be likened to anything known by man. Every concept of the divine nature that comes from comprehensible images and verbal discourse are poor approximations and meager guesses at what constitutes the divine nature. All are idols and do not proclaim the One True God.

Moses received the gift of divine illumination through the series of inner purification and contemplation as he ascended Mount Sinai. By gaining control over the passions and acquiring virtue, he purified his body and soul. Inner sanctification allowed him to leave behind the weaknesses of the flesh at the base of the mountain and begin the ascent of his soul to participation in the Divine Life[84]. As he ascended higher, the sound of the trumpet blast of the divine word became intelligible, which comes from the contemplation of reality and progress in the knowledge of divine power[85]. At the summit of the ascent, he was led into the inner sanctuary of divine knowledge where God

---

82   Gregory of Nyssa, *The Life of Moses*, 95 (II, 163).
83   *Ibid.*, 95-96 (II, 165).
84   *Ibid.*, 96 (II, 167).
85   *Ibid.*, 96-97 (II, 169).

is. The Scripture calls this "darkness", which signifies the unseen and unknown. Thus, the essence of God's nature is totally inaccessible to the created order. Nevertheless, the Divine Life is communicated by God through His energies, and perceived through spiritual senses acquired through the sacraments of the Church and ascetic purification[86].

From the summit, Moses passed on to the "tabernacle not made with human hands, that is, not of this creation" (Heb. 9:11), but which he showed to the Israelites at the base of the mountain by means of a material likeness (Exod. 25-27). The heavenly tabernacle, a mystery partially uncovered by the Apostle Paul, is Christ (Heb. 9:11). Therefore, man is allowed to perceive the One who transcends the creation through communion with Christ in the Holy Spirit[87], as the Holy Spirit declares to the believer what is Christ's and Who also abides in the believer forever (John 14:17; 16:12-15).

The life of Moses serves as a powerful example, emphasizing the truth that from each summit attained in the spiritual ascent to union with God, new horizons continually open up[88]. The stages of Moses's life are a pattern to be followed, a pattern characterized by the constant pursuit of achieving new heights in the spiritual ascent to God. Moses never stopped his ascent, nor did he ever set a limit for himself in his journey to God[89]. His life demonstrated the incessant transformation into the likeness of God as one stretches out toward the divine

---

[86] John Meyendorff, Preface to *Gregory of Nyssa: The Life of Moses*, xiii.

[87] *Ibid.*, xiii.

[88] Abraham J. Malherbe and Everett Ferguson, Introduction to *Gregory of Nyssa: The Life of Moses*, 12 (II, 226).

[89] Gregory of Nyssa, *The Life of Moses*, 113-114 (II, 227).

infinity, acquiring ever greater participation in God[90], "forgetting those things which are behind and reaching forward toward those things which are ahead" (Phil. 3:13).

Moses beseeched God to appear to him, not according to his own capacity to participate in the Divine Life, but according to God's true being[91]. Moses wanted to see God face to face (Exod. 33:18). God's response to this request is well summarized by St. Gregory of Nyssa: "The divine voice granted what was requested in what was denied, showing in a few words an immeasurable depth of thought"[92]. For the Lord said, "You cannot see My face; for no man can see My face and live ... You shall see My back; but My face shall not be seen" (Exod. 33:20, 23). The denial to see the face of God is understood in two ways. First, the one who thinks God is something to be known does not have life. The Divine Being is inaccessible to sense perception and intellectual knowledge[93]. Secondly, whatever stands face to face with true virtue stands opposite to virtue and is evil. Rather, participation in the Divine Life is attained by standing "on the rock" (Exod. 33:21) and beholding God as His "glory passes by" (Exod. 33:22). More precisely, from the "cleft of the rock," God is beheld by following Him wherever He might lead[94].

As observed from the life of Moses, the ascetic struggle to acquire virtue dilates the soul's capacity for virtue through exertion[95]. The journey of the soul to God is an eternal process. As St. Gregory of Nyssa observed, "he

---

90 *Ibid.,* 113 (II, 225).
91 *Ibid.,* 114 (II, 230).
92 *Ibid.,* 114-115 (II, 232).
93 *Ibid.,* 115 (II, 234-235)
94 *Ibid.,* 119-120 (II, 252-255).
95 *Ibid.,* 113 (II, 226).

[Moses] still thirsts for that with which constantly filled himself to capacity"[96]. The ascent to union with God is through perpetual progress in the virtuous life. This is seen through the divine word when the Lord told Moses that the path to participation in the glory of God is by following Him, by always keeping the back of God in view (Exod. 33:23; cf. Ps. 62:9). Yet, at the same time, ascent is achieved by standing still, for the Lord told Moses: "Here is a place by Me: you shall stand on the rock" (Exod. 33:21).

The notion of stillness may seem contradictory to advancement (Exod. 33:23). This passage is understood to mean that the eternal ascent to union with God is a dynamical process rooted in stability. The stability in the eternal ascent to union with God is based on the infinite Goodness of God, which is manifested by Christ, the "living stone" (1 Pet. 2:4-8), through His incarnation and sacrificial death (John 3:16; Matt. 26:26-29; 1 Pet. 2:21-25). There is never frustration or satiety in desiring God and participating in His divine life, but only the discovery of true Love[97]. As the holy Apostle exclaimed, "hope does not disappoint, because the love of God has been poured out in our hearts by the Holy Spirit who was given to us" (Rom. 5:5; cf. 8:38-39).

Moses achieved inner purification and the divine gift of illumination. He did not, however, attain theosis. His participation in the divine life was to such a great extent that his face radiated the glory of God (Exod. 34:29-35). Nevertheless, it was a fading glory (2 Cor. 3:7-8). The height of his contemplation was the vision of the heavenly tabernacle (Exod. 25:40), which revealed the mystery of

---

[96] *Ibid.*, 114 (II, 230).

[97] John Meyendorff, Preface to *Gregory of Nyssa: The Life of Moses*, xiv.

the Incarnation[98]. This is the limit of all such ascents in contemplation[99]. The image of the heavenly tabernacle not made with hands (Heb. 9:11), seen by Moses on the holy mountain, was given a material representation on earth, as instructed by God (Exod. 25:40). The tabernacle was both fashioned and un-fashioned, uncreated and pre-existing, but created in the sense of having received a material form[100]. The heavenly tabernacle, therefore, is the Only Begotten Son[101], who encompasses everything within Himself (Col. 1:15-17), but who also pitched His own tabernacle among us (John 1:14).

The place of theosis is within the tabernacle of God, made accessible to man through the incarnation of Jesus Christ. Christ united His divine nature to human nature (John 1:14). By uniting to Christ in baptism (Gal. 3:26-27), the believer becomes the tabernacle of God through the indwelling of the Holy Spirit (John 14:15-17; 1 Cor. 6:17; Eph. 2:19-22). The conversion of the soul through the mystery of baptism (and chrismation) restores man's capacity to reflect the image of God[102] (Ro. 6:3-11). The soul is continually purified by the Sacrament of Repentance (1 John 1:9; cf. John 20:21-23) and nourished by the Body and Blood of Christ in the Sacrament of the Eucharist (John 6:54; Luke 22:17-19, 28-30; 1 Cor. 10:14-17; 11:2730). The sacraments of the Church are made effectual for spiritual transformation by advancing in the personal ascetic struggle to acquire virtue through contemplation and inner purification. Progress in the ascetic struggle is

---

98   Gregory of Nyssa, *The Life of Moses*, 98-99 (II, 174-177).

99   *Ibid.*, 96 (II, 167).

100   *Ibid.*, 98 (II, 174).

101   *Ibid.*, 98-99 (II, 175).

102   *Ibid.*, 119 (II, 250-252).

a perpetual process. This precondition for theognosis was manifested in the life of Moses and reflected in the life of the Forerunner of the Christ (Matt. 11:11-15). That Jesus of Nazareth is the One through whom the believer is elevated to union with God through the deifying grace of the Holy Spirit is revealed at the Baptism of Christ in the Jordon.

The Holy Trinity is first revealed in the Gospel of St. Matthew at Jesus's baptism (Matt. 3:13-17). The revelation of the Trinity at this moment in the ministries of St. John and Jesus Christ is significant. The manifestation of the Holy Trinity at Christ's baptism simultaneously revealed that in the Person of the Divine Word, the Beloved Son, divinity and humanity are fully united. Furthermore, St. Matthew's account establishes the continuity between the ministries of St. John the Forerunner and Jesus. St. John's ministry was rooted in the episodes of Israel's exodus from Egypt, leading to the ascent of Moses on Mount Sinai, as previously discussed. By the unity of the divine and human natures in Christ, the baptism of Jesus purifies the creation and makes the waters effectual (sacramental) for the restoration of the image of God in man.

The baptism of Jesus and his ascetic struggles in the desert fulfilled all the typologies of Israel's flight from Egypt leading up to their encampment at the base of Mount Sinai (Matt. 4:1-11), bringing their accomplishments to perfection. In His humanity, Christ overcame the passions and achieved victory over temptation and the works of the devil, delighting and feeding on the wisdom of God and the joy of the Resurrection and Ascension into Heaven that He Himself would achieve (cf. Heb. 12:2). Light and Life had come into the world (John 1:1-5). In the Gospel of St. John the Evangelist, Jesus said: "I am the light of the world, He who follows Me shall not walk in darkness, but have the light of life" (John 8:12), which is a fulfillment of the prophetic word (Matt. 4:12-16; cf. Isa. 9:1-2).

With all the necessary preparation made ready by the Forerunner, with the purification of body and soul accomplished by the incarnation of Christ and the perfect synergy between His divine and human will, the time is at hand to ascend the mountain of God. The only appropriate response to the fulfillment of these things is recorded by St. Matthew: "From that time Jesus began to preach and to say: 'Repent, for the kingdom of God is at hand'" (Matt. 4:17).

At the base of the holy mountain, the divine invocation issued forth as Jesus called His first disciples. "Then He said to them, 'Follow Me'" (Matt. 4:19). This invocation refers to the divine word given to Moses when his deepest desire was to attain to ever greater participation in the Divine Life (Exod. 33:18-23). God told Moses to follow Him, from within the cleft of the Rock. This signifies an eternal pursuit of union made possible by the incarnation and the earthly ministry of Christ. Through Christ, the one who heeds the divine call to ascend the holy mountain will attain greater heights than Moses. Rather than a fading glory, "we all, with unveiled face, beholding as in a mirror the glory of the Lord, are being transformed into the same image from glory to glory, just as by the Spirit of the Lord... Therefore, if anyone is in Christ, he is a new creation; old things have passed away; behold all things have become new" (2 Cor. 3:18; 5:17).

Jesus Christ ascends the holy mountain and the trumpet blast of His voice proclaims the good tidings of the Gospel to all (Isa. 2:3; 40:9). In Him and through Him, union with the Holy Trinity is once again attainable to man, the pathway of which is to ascend the steps of Beatitudes leading to theosis.

O Lord, who shall dwell in Your tabernacle? Who shall live in Your holy mountain? He who walks blamelessly, and works righteousness, and speaks truth in his heart, who does not deceive with his tongue, neither does evil to his neighbor; and does not find fault with those nearest him. He disdains those who do evil in his presence, but he holds in honor those who fear the Lord; He swears an oath to his neighbor and does not set it aside. He does not lend his money at interest, and he does not take a bribe against the innocent. He who does these things shall never be shaken. (Ps 14).

Chapter 3: Blessed Are the Poor in Spirit

> Blessed are the poor in spirit, for theirs is the kingdom of heaven (Matt. 5:3).

Jesus interprets His preaching and healing ministry in terms of the prophetic word from Isaiah in chapter 61:1-7, which refers to the end-time redemption (cf., Matt. 11:4-6). Thus, Jesus's audience would have associated His ministry with the eschatological intervention of the Reign of God – i.e., the Kingdom of Heaven[103]. Moreover, the phrase "poor in spirit" in the first Beatitude (Matt. 5:3) is an explication of Isaiah 61:1-7, giving full range to the meaning of "poor" in the marcarism of Isaiah 61:1, which, in addition to its socioeconomic meaning, puts greater stress on the relationship of the "poor" to God. To summarize this relationship, the "poor in spirit" in the first Beatitude and the "poor" of Isaiah 61 are those who stand without pretense before God as their only hope. In the broader context of the gospel, and Jesus's teachings from the Sermon on the Mount in particular, the phrase "poor in spirit" can be adequately expressed by the word "humble"[104].

---

103 Hamm, *The Beatitudes in Context: What Luke and Matthew Meant*, 22-23.

104 *Ibid.*, 80-81. Hamm also cites the work of Dupont (in footnotes 11-12), who argues that "poor in spirit" is understood to mean

The Church Fathers also discerned that the "poor in spirit" in the Beatitudes are the "humble of spirit" or the "humble of heart." For example, St. Jerome noted that the first Beatitude (Matt. 5:3) is an elucidation of Isaiah 61:1, with blessedness associated more with humility than with poverty[105]. St. Hilary of Poitiers said the prophets anticipated the first Beatitude as humility of spirit when they announced that God would choose a people humble and in awe of His words[106] (Isa. 66:2). As the Psalmist said, "He [God] will save the humble in spirit" (Ps. 33:19). St. John Chrysostom added that "poor in spirit" is humility and contrition of mind and spirit[107].

Poverty of spirit, indeed, is a virtue to be congratulated. It is a disposition that prepares the soul to receive and experience the blessedness of the kingdom of God. Detachment from all that stains the soul enables it to be filled with God who is purity, immortality, light, and truth[108]. In the words of Jesus, "unless you are converted and become as little children, you will by no means enter the kingdom of heaven. Therefore, whoever humbles himself as this little child is the greatest in the kingdom of heaven" (Matt. 18:3-4). The word "spirit" in the first

---

"humble" from textual analysis of the Hebrew parallel of Matt. 5:3 found in a Qumran document (1QM 14:7).

105 Jerome, *Ancient Christian Commentary on Scripture: New Testament Ia; Matthew 1-13*, ed. Manlio Simonetti (Downers Grove, IL: InterVarsity Press, 2001), 81.

106 St. Hilary of Poitiers, *Ancient Christian Commentary on Scripture: New Testament Ia; Matthew 1-13*, ed. Manlio Simonetti (Downers Grove, IL: InterVarsity Press, 2001), 81.

107 Chrysostom, "Homily XV: Matt. V. 1,2", in *Nicene and Post-Nicene Fathers*, 92.

108 Hilda C. Graef, introduction to *The Lord's Prayer, The Beatitudes*, by St. Gregory of Nyssa, 17.

Beatitude qualifies the word "poor" by designating the soul and its faculty of choice[109]. For the poor in spirit are those who willingly and freely humbly themselves in response to the Holy Spirit[110].

Defining poverty of spirit in terms of humility requires some important provisos. It cannot mean humility simply in terms of submission and a lowly external state, as explained by St. John Chrysostom[111]. Poverty of spirit is a disposition not only of submissiveness, but of utter brokenness (e.g., Ps. 50:17; the Song of the Three Holy Children in Dan. 3:39). It is from the condition of utter inner brokenness that poverty of spirit forms a sure foundation, for which an encounter with God will result in a favorable judgement and lead to union with Him. In His usage of the language from the prophet Isaiah, Jesus employs the phrase "poor in spirit" rather than "humble" to emphasize the interior attitudes of those who are awestruck by God and tremble at His commandments (Isa. 66:2).

Pride is the root and origin of all wickedness (1 Tim. 3:6; see also 1 John 2:16). The vice of arrogance is ingrained in almost everyone who shares human nature[112]. Christ said in the Gospel, "whoever exalts himself will be humbled, and he who humbles himself will be exalted" (Luke 14:11). The root of all evil, therefore, is pride. But the root of all good, on the other hand, is humility[113]. On this basis, Sts.

---

109 Chrysostom, "Homily XV: Matt. V. 1,2", in *Nicene and Post-Nicene Fathers*, 92.

110 Jerome, *Ancient Christian Commentary on Scripture: New Testament Ia; Matthew 1-13*, 81.

111 Chrysostom, "Homily XV: Matt. V. 1,2", in *Nicene and Post-Nicene Fathers*, 92.

112 St. Gregory of Nyssa, *The Lord's Prayer, The Beatitudes*, 91.

113 Anonymous, *Ancient Christian Commentary on Scripture: New Testament Ia; Matthew 1-13*, 81.

John Chrysostom and Gregory of Nyssa both concluded that poverty of spirit is a suitable remedy to the disease of pride[114]. The first step in sanctification, to root out pride and gain control of the passions, is to choose humility and engage in the ascetic struggle to nurture its growth.

Developing the virtue of humility is the beginning stage of inner purification. With reference to the typologies of the Israelite's exodus from Egypt discussed in chapter 2, the believer is placed on the pathway of salvation through the mystical waters of baptism. The seed of sanctification implanted in the Christian through the Sacrament of Baptism grows by following the two guides: the life of Jesus Christ revealed by the indwelling Holy Spirit (John 14:6, 15-17; 16:14-15). This first Beatitude is the first rung in the ladder of the step-by-step pathway leading to theosis. The passage from Isaiah in chapter 66:2, which identifies the theanthropic Body of Christ as the means of access to God, lists humility and peace as those virtues by which one participates in the Divine Word made flesh. Humility and peace are also the virtues that correspond to the first and last of the seven Beatitudes[115] (Matt. 5:3, 9). With the number seven representing fullness of divinity in ancient Hebrew number symbolism[116], the correspondence between the passage from Isaiah and the first and seventh of the Beatitudes also indicates that they are to be understood as a step-by-step process of assimilation of virtue, leading to communion with God.

---

114   Chrysostom, "Homily XV: Matt. V. 1,2", in *Nicene and Post-Nicene Fathers*, 92; St. Gregory of Nyssa, *The Lord's Prayer, The Beatitudes*, 91.

115   *Ibid.*, 92.

116   Paul Nadim Tarazi, *The New Testament: Introduction; Vol. 3; Johannine Writings* (Crestwood, NY: St. Vladimir's Seminary Press, 2004), 22-25.

As discussed in the Introduction chapter, the Beatitudes express the two complementary ways of theognosis. Blessed Augustin noticed that a succinct revelation of cataphatic theology is the ladder of theophanies given by the sevenfold operation of the Holy Spirit in the divine economy: wisdom, understanding, counsel, might, knowledge, godliness, and the fear of God (Isa. 11:2-3). This listing proceeds from the more excellent degrees of God's energies to the lesser degrees, in order that the follower of Christ may ascend this ladder in the reverse order[117]. Ascending this ladder is achieved by assimilating the Beatitudes in an apophatic approach based on the imitation of Christ and the deifying grace of the Holy Spirit (Gal. 3:27; 4:4-6; 2 Cor. 5:17; Eph. 2:1-10).

The fear of God is the last (lowest) in the list of the operations of the Holy Spirit, while wisdom is the first (highest) (Isa. 11:2-3). On the other hand, "the fear of God is the beginning of wisdom" (Prov. 1:7). Thus, there is a ladder of virtue to be climbed in the ascent to greater participation in the higher energies of God. At the beginning of the spiritual ascent, the follower of Christ must develop a sense of awe before God and tremble at His words (Isa. 66:2) before advancing to greater virtue. Developing the fear of God brings about inner purification, leading to participation in the eternity of the Divine Life. As the Psalmist said, "the fear of God is pure, enduring unto ages of ages" (Ps. 18:10). Therefore, the "fear of God" in the seven-fold operation of the Holy Spirit corresponds to the "poor in spirit" in the first Beatitude. As the Apostle Paul said, "do not be haughty, but fear" (Rom. 11:20). The "poor in spirit" stand before God in deep humility, beyond intellections about God, in the earnest hope that that He is

---

117 Augustin, "Our Lord's Sermon on the Mount: Book I", in *Nicene and Post-Nicene Fathers*, 6.

very Light, Life, and Salvation: "The Lord is my light and my savior; whom shall I fear? The Lord is the defender of my life; whom shall I dread?" (Ps. 26:1).

Humility is not only the first step in achieving inner purification in the journey to union with God, but it is also the first step in the contemplation of God. The first stage in the contemplation of the Divine Life is the realization that God Himself is humble. The Incarnation of Christ manifests the humility of God (Phil. 2:5-11). In the Gospel Jesus said, "Come to Me, all you who labor and are heavy laden, and I will give you rest. Take My yoke upon you and learn from Me, for I am gentle and lowly in heart, and you will find rest for your souls. For My yoke is easy and My burden is light" (Matt. 11:28-30). Sin and vice weigh the soul down in the ascent to communion with God (e.g., Heb. 12:1-2). Humility, as virtue, is light and lifts the soul upward towards God. Therefore, let us become poor in spirit that we may ascend to greater heights toward theosis[118].

Inner purification and the contemplation of God are intricately linked (1 Pet.1:15-16), as previously stated. Christ revealed and manifested the seven-fold operation of the Holy Spirit by His incarnation, illuminating the pathway to participation in the Divine Life through imitation of Him (e.g. John 14:6; 17:3). Christ manifested the "fear of God" (Isa. 11:2-3) in the flesh during His earthly ministry by submitting to the authority of the Father and by saying only what the Father told Him (John 12:49-50), by doing only the work of the Father (John 5:19-21), and by submitting His human will to His divine will at the Garden of Gethsemane before His Passion and Crucifixion (Matt. 26:36-48). Moreover, Jesus taught that the humbleness of God is incarnated each time the follower of Christ

---

118   St. Gregory of Nyssa, *The Lord's Prayer, The Beatitudes*, 95.

suffers injustice by turning the other cheek, by going the extra mile, by giving to those who ask and cannot repay, and by praying for one's enemies and doing good to the unlovely (Matt. 5:38-48). Christ demonstrated all these manifestations of humility in His earthly ministry, and especially in His Passion and Crucifixion as succinctly summarized by the Apostle Peter (1 Pet. 2:21-25). Humility is the natural disposition of the one who possesses the fear of God.

Participation in the Divine Life and imitation of Christ go hand in hand[119] (John 14:23). Participation (*methexsis* in Greek) is a philosophical term employed to express the composite teachings on theosis from Scripture and from the Church Fathers in a compact way. It means "sharing in the attributes of another"[120]. The operation of the Holy Spirit is to declare the divine glory and goodness of God through the prophetic word (Isa. 11:2-3), and to enable the believer to recognize the divinity of the incarnate Christ (John 16:14-15). By imitating Christ, through the assimilation of the Beatitudes as a succinct embodiment of the life of Christ, the humanity of the follower of Christ is taken into the Divine Life and deified through the grace of the Holy Spirit (John 14:17), thereby manifesting the glory and goodness of God (2 Cor. 3:18). This relationship between imitation and participation is derived from the teachings of the Apostle Paul: "For you know the grace of our Lord Jesus Christ, that though He was rich, yet for your sakes He became poor, that you through His poverty might become rich" (2 Cor. 8:9). Therefore, the first step in participation in the Divine Life, in advancing along the pathway to theosis, is to imitate the humility of Christ.

---

119 Russell, *Fellow Workers with God: Orthodox Thinking on Theosis*, 27.

120 *Ibid.*, 127.

The apophatic approach to acquiring virtue is opposed to a spirit of complacency or any other form of limit. The riches of virtue must be pursued with a zealous, dynamic quest for spiritual wealth[121] (Matt. 6:19). The examples of the humility of Christ in the Gospels serve as a guide, a stepping stone by which the follower of Christ can expand his soul toward the infinite humility of God. Participation also means possessing what is not self-caused, which is the strong sense of the philosophical word[122]. The strong sense of participation draws on the Apostle Paul's teaching on participatory union with Christ through baptism (Rom. 6:3-11). The Sacraments of the Church establish the ontological relationship between the believer and the Holy Trinity, which recreates and revivifies the soul in the newness of life (Rom. 6:4; 2 Cor. 5:17). This newness of life opens boundless horizons to assimilate the virtue of humility. The soul is incessantly presented with the choice between humility and arrogance, or humility and pride[123]. The drive to acquire virtue is a movement of love. The soul reaches beyond its current capacity for humility, or any virtue, in ecstasy, which is a going out of the self under the impulse of love[124]. This movement of love is reciprocated by God as He Himself goes out in ecstasy to meet the believer. Union with God is the product of divine *eros*, where the lovers strive to be united with the object of their longing. Theosis is not union with the transcendent essence of God, but with the perceptible radiance of His glory and goodness by which He presents Himself to mankind. Grounded in

---

121 St. Gregory of Nyssa, *The Lord's Prayer, The Beatitudes,* 89.

122 Russell, *Fellow Workers with God: Orthodox Thinking on Theosis,* 127-128.

123 Gregory of Nyssa, *The Life of Moses,* 58 (II, 14-15).

124 Russell, *Fellow Workers with God: Orthodox Thinking on Theosis,* 118, 144-145.

the true freedom of love, assimilating the virtue of humility has no limit.

Perfect love establishes the believer in the likeness of Christ (1 John 3:16). The purpose and complete fulfillment of divine eros is the vision (*theoria*) of the Divine Life and union with it[125] (1 John 4:8-16). Love intertwines the soul with God in mutual embrace[126]. Love creates in a mystical fashion a pure and holy co-existence of the human with the Divine Life (John 17:24-26). Love is the impulse that undergirds the constant effort to imitate the example of love given to us by Jesus Christ (John 13:34-35; Eph. 5:1-2). The pathway to theosis is to participate in the only true life, the Holy Trinity, which is the supreme perfection, the only True Love[127]. "For God so loved the world that He gave His Only-Begotten Son" (John 3:16). The first stage of the fulfillment and perfection of God's love in the divine economy is the humility of God manifested in the Incarnation of the Son of God. Therefore, the first step in participating in the Divine Life is by imitating the love of God revealed by Christ in the self-emptying (*kenosis*) and humility of His earthly ministry (Phil. 2:5-11).

Although poverty of spirit is the first step in the development of virtue, participation in the kingdom of God is promised even at this beginning stage in the spiritual ascent to theosis. "For theirs is the kingdom of heaven" (Matt. 5:3) is in the present tense[128]. Voluntary poverty in wickedness, but fervent in spirit, lays up treasure in heaven[129]. The Beatific Vision, the vision and knowledge

---

125 Stavropoulos, *Partakers of Divine Nature*, 83.

126 *Ibid.*, 83.

127 *Ibid.*, 90.

128 Hamm, *The Beatitudes in Context: What Luke and Matthew Meant*, 83-84.

129 St. Gregory of Nyssa, *The Lord's Prayer, The Beatitudes*, 89.

of God, is the highest attainment of life in Heaven[130], a fruit of the Kingdom of God. Thus, the Beatitude of the "poor in spirit" is that the perfect and highest attainment of the human soul is in some degree accessible at the very beginning of the journey to union with God[131].

> Behold, the eyes of the Lord are on those who fear Him, on those who hope in His mercy, to deliver their souls from death and to keep them alive in famine. Our soul shall wait for the Lord; He is our helper and protector; for our heart shall be glad in Him, and we hope in His holy name. Let Your mercy, O Lord, be upon us, as we hope in You (Ps. 32:18-22).

---

[130] Hilda C. Graef, introduction to *The Lord's Prayer, The Beatitudes*, by St. Gregory of Nyssa, 18.

[131] Augustin, "Our Lord's Sermon on the Mount: Book I", in *Nicene and Post-Nicene Fathers*, 7.

Chapter 4:
Blessed Are Those Who Mourn

Blessed are those who mourn, for they shall be comforted (Matt. 5:4).

Having attained some measure of humility (Ps. 32:18-22), having had tasted in some small way the blessed fruit of the kingdom of God (Ps. 33:10-11), the follower of Christ is led by the grace of the Holy Spirit to the next step in the ascent to union with God (Ps. 142:10). The believer arrives next at blessed mourning. The second Beatitude corresponds to the sixth operation of the Holy Spirit in the descending order of the ladder of theophanies listed in Isaiah 11:2-3, which is "godliness"[132]. The reason blessed

---

[132] Augustin, "Our Lord's Sermon on the Mount: Book I", in *Nicene and Post-Nicene Fathers*, 5-6. It is important to note that Augustin reverses the order of the listing of the Beatitudes of mourning and meekness compared to modern translations of the Beatitudes in the Gospel of St. Matthew. Refer to footnote 1, page 5 in this volume of the *Nicene and Post-Nicene Fathers*. Scholars believe Augustin's ordering follows the Codex Sinaiticus ("Sinai Bible") manuscript. Codex Sinaiticus was one of the fifty copies of the Bible commissioned from Eusebius by Emperor Constantine. There were separate scribes who copied the work, and whose copies are designated A, B, C, D. Augustin is believed to have used Codex D. Gregory of Nyssa also followed Augustin's ordering of mourning and meekness in *The Lord's Prayer, The Beatitudes*, 97, 106, presumably for a similar reason. See also Hamm, *The Beatitudes in Context*, 86-87. The Latin Vulgate also has mourning following meekness in the ordering

mourning is identified with godliness is because this form of sorrow refers to mourning over sin, according to Sts. Jerome and John Chrysostom[133], and the blessedness of mourning is that "godly sorrow produces repentance leading to salvation" (2 Cor. 7:10).

Blessed mourning comes as the result of some healing word from Scripture, whether heard or read, that is received like painful surgery or bitter medicine[134]. This type of medicinal word uncovers and exposes personal sin and speaks of the fierce threats of the Judgment to come:

---

of the Beatitudes in St. Matthew's Gospel. It is believed that scribes, such as the translators of Codex D, reversed the order to exploit the rhetorical antithesis between heaven and earth in the blessedness promised to the poor in spirit and the meek, respectively. However, the order of the beatitudes of mourning and meekness in modern translations is aligned with Isaiah 61, suggesting that this was the original ordering given by St. Matthew. The author of this book kept the order of the Beatitudes according to modern English translations, which means the correspondence of mourning and meekness with the seven-fold operations of the Holy Spirit (Isa. 11:2-3) is reversed with respect to Augustin. It is this author's belief that the words used to describe the operations of the Holy Spirit in Isaiah 11:2-3 are sufficiently broad to encompass either ordering of the Beatitudes of mourning and meekness.

133   Jerome and Chrysostom, *Ancient Christian Commentary on Scripture: New Testament Ia; Matthew 1-13*, 81-82. We are helped in discerning the meaning of mourning in the Beatitudes listed in the Gospel of St. Matthew by comparing the woe on those who laugh in Luke 7:22. In this passage of St. Luke's Gospel, Jesus issues a woe upon those who are satisfied with earthly things and avoid the seriousness of repentance. See footnote 3 in Augustin, "Our Lord's Sermon on the Mount: Book I", in *Nicene and Post-Nicene Fathers*, 5. The association of mourning in the second Beatitude with sin and unrepentance is further strengthened by the passage from James 4:7-10. St. James appears to be expounding upon the second Beatitude recorded in the Gospels (Matt. 5:4 and Luke 7:22).

134   St. Gregory of Nyssa, *The Lord's Prayer, The Beatitudes*, 108.

for example, the terror of hell and unquenchable fire, of the worm that does not die, the perpetual weeping and gnashing of teeth, and the expulsion of the soul to outer darkness (cf. Matt. 8:12; 22:13, 30; Mark 9:43; Luke 13:28; Jude 7, 13). The Apostle aptly describes this type of divine word:

> For the word of God is living and powerful, and sharper than any two-edged sword, piercing even to the division of soul and spirit, and of joints and marrow, and is a discerner of the thoughts and intents of the heart. And there is no creature hidden from His sight, but all things are naked and open to the eyes of Him to whom we must give account (Heb. 4:12-13).

Blessed mourning is vividly demonstrated when the Apostle Peter preached the gospel to the nations on the Day of Pentecost:

> "Therefore let all the house of Israel know assuredly that God has made this Jesus, whom you crucified, both Lord and Christ." Now when they heard this they were cut to the heart, and said to Peter and the rest of the apostles, "Men and brethren, what shall we do?" Then Peter said to them, "Repent, and let every one of you be baptized in the name of Jesus Christ for the remission of sins; and you shall receive the gift of the Holy Spirit. For the promise is to you and to your children, and to all who are afar off, as many as the Lord our God will call" (Acts 2:36-39).

The above passages from Scripture express the depth and intensity of this form of sorrow. This is the reason

Jesus used the word "mourning" rather than "sorrow" in the Beatitudes. To mourn is to sorrow intensely[135]. The blessedness of this mourning is not the painful experience or the sorrow in and of itself, but rather that the divine word was received as medicine by a humble spirit, leading to the forgiveness of sins and to the healing work of salvation (Acts 2:38; 2 Cor. 7:10). This Beatitude is profitable at all stages of development in the virtuous life. Until the theanthropic Body of Christ attains theosis (Eph. 3:14-19; 4:13-16), the human nature of the believer on earth is afflicted with sin (1 John 1:8), the remedy of which is the blessed sorrow of repentance[136]. From the first epistle of St. John, "if we confess our sins, He is faithful to forgive our sins and to cleanse us from all unrighteousness" (1 John 1:9).

St. John Chrysostom also reasoned that blessed mourning is a perpetual benefit in the spiritual life of the believer because of its potential to develop other virtues. Godly sorrow that produces repentance can teach self-control[137]. For example, those who grieve the loss of loved ones in this earthly life have no desire for gain or pleasure. They are not given over to vainglory. Nor are they provoked by insults, beset with envy, or seized by any other passion. Consequently, those who mourn for their sins ought to show forth a self-denial even greater than this.

Moses prescribed unleavened bread for the feast of Passover and bitter herbs for seasoning (Exod. 12:8). St. Gregory of Nyssa says that this teaches us that the

---

135 Chrysostom, "Homily XV: Matt. V. 1,2", in *Nicene and Post-Nicene Fathers*, 93.

136 St. Gregory of Nyssa, *The Lord's Prayer, The Beatitudes*, 108.

137 Chrysostom, "Homily XV: Matt. V. 1,2", in *Nicene and Post-Nicene Fathers*, 93.

follower of Christ cannot participate in the mystical feast of the Kingdom of God without voluntarily mixing the bitter herbs of earthly life, in addition to the simple and unleavened life[138] (cf., John 16:33). Blessed Augustin said that mourning in the second Beatitude is sorrow arising from the loss of things held dear[139]. Those who have been converted to God lose those things which they were accustomed to embrace as valuable in the world. Until the love for eternal things is firmly established in their souls, they are wounded by some measure of grief. As discussed in Chapter 2, life removed from the passions and the pleasures of evil seem difficult at the beginning of the virtuous life. Recalling from Chapter 2 the spiritual meaning of the bitter waters of Marah, the twelve fountains and seventy palm trees at Elim, and the manna from heaven, the spiritual sojourner is refreshed by the Gospel teachings and nourished by the Sacrament of the Eucharist, and the difficult struggle to acquire virtue is made sweet by the hope of the resurrection. The blessed comfort received from these "exceedingly great and precious promises" (2 Pet. 1:4) is the Comforter Himself, the Holy Spirit.

The mystery of the Lord's Incarnation and His earthly ministry was revealed by Jesus in His discourses during the Last Supper, as recorded in the Gospel of St. John: "It is to your advantage that I go away; for if I do not go away, the Helper will not come to you; but if I depart, I will send Him to you... He will glorify Me, for He will take what is Mine and declare it to you. All things that the Father has are Mine. Therefore, I said that He will take of Mine and declare it to you... And I will pray the Father, and He will give you another Helper, that He may abide with you

---

138   St. Gregory of Nyssa, *The Lord's Prayer, The Beatitudes*, 115.

139   Augustin, "Our Lord's Sermon on the Mount: Book I", in *Nicene and Post-Nicene Fathers*, 5.

forever – the Spirit of Truth (John 16:7, 14-15; 14:14:16-17). Blessed Augustin said that the exceedingly great and precious promises to those who mourn their sins is that they will participate in the Divine Life through the comfort of the Holy Spirit Himself, "while losing the temporal joy, they may enjoy to the full that which is eternal"[140].

Since Jesus Christ is the perfect revelation of godliness and the perfect embodiment of virtue (cf. Heb. 1:3), how can one imitate the sinless Christ in blessed mourning? There are two ways. First, Christ mourned the sins of others and the sorrowful consequences that the Fall has introduced into the created order. A few examples from the Gospels are the following. Jesus wept over the city of Jerusalem after His triumphal entry. The peace that Israel sought was before their eyes. But because of their sins, they did not recognize their Messiah, and they were soon going to kill Him (Luke 19:41-44). In addition, Jesus wept bitterly over the death of His beloved friend Lazarus (John 11:33-35). He wept over the sorrow that death brings, over the disfigurement and utter disintegration that the Fall and individual sin has introduced into a world created good. St. John Chrysostom also concluded that the follower of Christ must not only mourn his own sin but the sins of others. Examples of this virtue were also manifested by Moses, David, and the Apostle Paul[141].

The second way to imitate Christ in acquiring blessed mourning is to transform the sinful state and its effects into new life. Through the incarnation of Christ, God has journeyed into the very depths of human existence[142]. From

---

140   *Ibid.*, 5.

141   Chrysostom, "Homily XV: Matt. V. 1,2", in *Nicene and Post-Nicene Fathers*, 93.

142   Metropolitan Philip (Saliba) and Joseph Allen, *Meeting*

the depths which one cries in mourning is a cry emerging from God's own life already present from within (cf. Ps. 41:8; 129:1-8). Although Christ is without sin, He became sin for us, and was tempted in all the ways that we are (Heb. 4:15-16; 2 Cor. 5:21). Through His Passion, Death, and Resurrection, the ultimate defeat of humanity by sin, which is death, has been transformed by Christ into victory, a transition to eternal life, a passage into the Kingdom of God (1 Cor. 15:54-57; Rom. 6:3-11). The Resurrection of Christ is in the depths of the believer through the indwelling Holy Spirit[143] (Phil. 3:7-11). With death defeated by Christ, the immediacy of the divinity of life is revealed[144] (Phil. 1:21). In everyday living, the resurrection of Christ gives His followers the freedom and power to confront every obstacle to human existence in a fallen world, just as the Apostle Paul proclaims (Rom. 8:35-39; 1 Cor. 15:58): the freedom to confront life, death, tribulation and distress, the powers of the cosmos, the present and the future.

Jesus Christ lived through all the spiritual dimensions of everyday human existence (Heb. 2:10-18), and He continually lives in the depths of His followers through the Holy Spirit (John 14:15-17; Heb. 9:14; 10:15-23; Col. 1:27). Through the comfort of the Holy Spirit, the imitation of the Passion of Christ transforms mourning into greater desire for and participation in the Kingdom of God (2 Cor. 1:3-7). The Apostle summarized it well: "looking unto Jesus, the author and finisher of our faith, who for the joy that was set before Him enduring the cross, despising the shame, and has sat down at the right hand of the throne of

---

the Incarnate God: From the Human Depths to the Mystery of Fidelity (Brookline, MA: Holy Cross Orthodox Press, 2009), 5-6, 13.

143   *Ibid.,* 45.

144   *Ibid.,* 43-44.

God" (Heb. 12:2). This is the apophatic disposition required to extend beyond the present conflict with sin to a greater participation in the Kingdom of God.

St. Gregory of Nyssa also developed an apophatic vision of acquiring the virtue of blessed mourning. He noticed that the Beatitude refers to one who is always mourning, requiring a continual, deeper response to the revelation of God in Christ, in contrast to repentance over specific infractions of God's eternal Law[145]. St. Gregory takes his cue from the prophet Habakkuk: "The Lord God is my strength; He will direct my feet to the end; He will set me upon high places, so to conquer by His song" (Hab. 3:19). By contemplating the glory of Jesus Christ and the deeper reflection on the meaning of mourning, the believer is propelled to greater desire for participation in the Divine Life. Mourning is a painful sensation caused by the privation of something pleasant. Having attained some measure of inner purification through humility and godly sorrow, the promised Beatific Vision, even if seen only dimly, enables man to perceive the true good. As a result, the soul will be in distress, realizing the current poverty of human nature [146]. Blessed Augustin said that at this stage the soul begins to know the entanglements to which it is held by carnal desire; thus; the loss of the highest good (Paradise, communion with God) is mourned over[147]. The virtue one sees in Christ is the virtue which man once possessed in Paradise.

When Jesus calls mourning blessed, the soul of His followers should be compelled to turn to the true good

---

[145] St. Gregory of Nyssa, *The Lord's Prayer, The Beatitudes*, 108-109.

[146] *Ibid.*, 110-111.

[147] Augustin, "Our Lord's Sermon on the Mount: Book I", in *Nicene and Post-Nicene Fathers*, 6.

and not to immerse oneself in the deceits and passions of the present life[148]. As St. Gregory said, "but if man does not seek, he will not find what comes only to those who seek. For this reason, the Word calls mourning blessed" (cf. Matt. 7:7-8). This desire and the striving for the true good is the beginning of godliness (cf. Isa. 11:2-3). Moreover, the sojourner is not frustrated nor confounded by the ascetic struggle in the ascent to theosis, for he has been given the comfort of the Holy Spirit for the journey.

> O Lord, do not reprove me in Your anger, nor discipline me in Your wrath. Have mercy on me, O Lord, for I am weak; Heal me, O Lord, for my bones are troubled; and my soul is greatly troubled... Every single night I will dampen my bed; I will drench my couch with my tears... For the Lord heard the voice of my weeping; The Lord heard my supplication; The Lord received my prayer (Ps. 6:12-4, 7, 9-10).

---

148   *Ibid.*, 114-115.

Chapter 5:
Blessed Are the Meek

Blessed are the meek, for they shall inherit the earth (Matt. 5:5)

At this stage in the ascent to union with God, the follower of Christ has acquired the strength to gain some victory over sin. The virtue that conquers the passions is meekness[149]. Meekness is developed by putting the knowledge of the gospel into action[150]. "Knowledge" is the fifth operation of the Holy Spirit in the descending order of the ladder of theophanies given in Isaiah 11:2-3, which corresponds to this third Beatitude. In terms of the symbols and typologies represented by the historical events of the Israelite's exodus from Egypt analyzed in chapter 2, progress in advancing to the virtue of meekness can be summarized as follows. The spiritual sojourner who is nourished by the Sacraments of the Church, who follows Christ in the Holy Spirit, who has been strengthened and refreshed by the gospel teachings, and has acquired a fervent desire for the true good, is able to gain victory in the battle with sin and the passions, just as the Israelites had matured to the stage of being victorious in the battle with Amalek.

In the Septuagint, the word "meek" is a translation of

---

149 St. Gregory of Nyssa, *The Lord's Prayer, The Beatitudes*, 100-103.

150 Chromatius, *Ancient Christian Commentary on Scripture: New Testament Ia; Matthew 1-13*, 82.

the Greek word *prays* (the plural form in the Beatitudes is *praeis*), which occurs only once in the OT. It is found in the description of Moses in Numbers 12:3: "Now the man Moses was very *meek*, more than all men on the face of the earth." In the context of this passage, Miriam and Aaron spoke against Moses because he married a foreign woman. Moses did not retaliate but left judgment to God. Because of the wickedness of Miriam and Aaron, the Lord afflicted Miriam with leprosy. Rather than being vindictive, Moses pleaded with God to have mercy on Miriam and heal her. God heard Moses's prayer. For this reason, the Church Fathers describe the meek as gentle persons who neither provoke evil nor are provoked by evil[151]. The meek one is more content to endure an offense than to commit one. The person who is truly meek neither does evil nor thinks of doing evil when offended. Chromatius said that the meek are gentle, humble, and unassuming, simple in faith and patient in the face of every affront[152].

St. Gregory of Nyssa elucidates the rich meaning of the word "meek" by describing its various manifestations[153]. Meekness is a regulator against the impulse toward evil; meekness moderates the passions. The absolute absence of the passions is contrary to human nature, even in its perfected state. Meekness, on the other hand, is the virtue that prevents desire from overcoming the will. The work of the virtue of meekness is not to be carried away by the impulse of passion as by a torrent. St. Gregory provides his own macarism concerning meekness: "Blessed, therefore, are those who are not easily turned towards the passionate

---

151 Anonymous, *Ancient Christian Commentary on Scripture: New Testament Ia; Matthew 1-13*, 83.

152 Chromatius, *Ancient Christian Commentary on Scripture: New Testament Ia; Matthew 1-13*, 82.

153 St. Gregory of Nyssa, *The Lord's Prayer, The Beatitudes*, 100-103.

movements of the soul, but who are steadied by reason."[154] Here, reason is the "Spirit of knowledge" acquired as meekness (Isa. 11:2-3).

The word "meek" occurs rarely in the NT also. The word appears twice in St. Matthew's Gospel[155]. The first occurrence is in Matthew 11:28-29: "Come to Me, all you who labor and are heavy laden, and I will give you rest. Take My yoke upon you and learn from Me, for I am *gentle* and *lowly* in heart, and you will find rest for your souls." The adjectives "gentle" and "lowly" (or "humble") in this passage, and "meek" from Numbers 12:3, are all translations of the Greek word *prays* discussed above. There are two important points concerning the above passage from the Gospel of St. Matthew. First, Jesus is meekness incarnate. For the follower of Christ, meekness is acquired by the grace of the Holy Spirit through the imitation of Christ's meekness. Secondly, this passage reveals the mystery of the journey to theosis. Rest is experienced in shouldering the yoke of the ascetic struggle to acquire virtue and overcome sin; joy is known in the very cost of following Christ. These two points are elaborated below.

Armed with the precepts of the Gospel, the meek imitate the meekness of Christ[156]. Christ embodied and manifested all aspects of meekness discussed above. The Apostle Peter, an eyewitness to the Passion of Christ, said it this way:

> For to this you were called, because Christ also suffered for us, leaving us an example, that you

---

154   *Ibid.*, 103.

155   Hamm, *The Beatitudes in Context: What Luke and Matthew Meant*, 89-90.

156   Chromatius, *Ancient Christian Commentary on Scripture: New Testament Ia; Matthew 1-13*, 82.

> should follow His steps: "Who committed no sin, nor was deceit found in His mouth", who, when He was reviled, did not revile in return; when He suffered, He did not threaten, but committed Himself to Him who judges righteously; who Himself bore our sins in His own body on the tree, that we, having died to sins, might live for righteousness – by whose stripes you were healed. For you were like sheep going astray, but have now returned to the Shepherd and Overseer of your souls (1 Pet. 2:21-25).

The meekness of Christ overcame the passions of human nature and penetrated to the very depths of human existence and defeated the final enemy, death itself (1 Cor. 15:55-56).

The other occurrence of the word "meek" in the Gospel of St. Matthew is in chapter 21:5: "Tell the daughter of Zion, 'Behold, your King is coming to you, *lowly* [*prays*], and sitting on a donkey, a colt, the foal of a donkey.'" The context of this passage is Jesus's triumphal entry into Jerusalem, in fulfillment of the prophetic word of Isaiah 62:11 and Zechariah 9:9. The remainder of the prophet's vision (Zech. 9:10) includes the paradox of a conquering king with a dis-arming dominion over the whole earth[157]. This episode in Jesus's ministry is key to understanding the third Beatitude for two reasons, as explained below.

First, Jesus conquers by meekness. Jesus comes into the possession of the land non-violently, as an unexpectedly peaceful king[158]. This point is further strengthened by

---

157 Hamm, *The Beatitudes in Context: What Luke and Matthew Meant*, 90.

158 *Ibid.*, 90-91. It is interesting to note that Jesus, the Son of David, conquered Zion in exactly the opposite way that King David

noting the two mountain scenes that provide bookends to St. Matthew's Gospel. Jesus defeated temptation by telling the devil that the Son of God will come into His inheritance by obedience to the Father (Matt. 3:15, 17). Moreover, by demonstrating His sonship in the defeat of death on the Cross, the risen Son of God said in the final mountain scene, "All authority has been given to Me in heaven and on earth" (Matt. 28:18). Jesus came into His inheritance, not by gasping for it, but by casting His soul into the hands of the Father (1 Pet. 2:23). Thus, the meek one inherits the earth!

The second reason why Matthew 21:5 is key to understanding the third Beatitude is that this passage reveals clearly the meaning of inheriting the earth. Inheriting the earth is a symbol for the Kingdom of God, which is experienced in the present and is also the reward of the New Aeon[159]. St. John Chrysostom places emphasis on the present, sensible blessing for the meek suggested by the inheritance of land[160]. He cites many examples where Christ mingles spiritual with sensible promises and fulfilments, including examples from the Sermon on the Mount. St. Gregory of Nyssa, on the other hand, refers to the inherited land in the third Beatitude as the supercelestial earth[161],

---

originally did a millennium earlier. David acquired Jerusalem by force (2 Kgs. 5:6-12). In response to Jebusite mocking, David said, "The blind and the lame shall not come into the house of the Lord" (2 Kgs. 5:8). On the contrary, when Jesus entered the Temple as the Son of David, "the blind and lame came to Him in the temple, and He healed them" (Matt. 21:14). Thus, Jesus, the Son of David, is inaugurating a new way to come into the inheritance of God, a way of peace and non-violence.

159 *Ibid.*, 91-92.

160 Chrysostom, "Homily XV: Matt. V. 1,2", in *Nicene and Post-Nicene Fathers*, 93.

161 St. Gregory of Nyssa, *The Lord's Prayer, The Beatitudes*, 97, 99-100.

placing more weight on the eschatological reward for the meek. He draws upon the Psalms that speak of the "land of the living", a land where death does not approach, the wicked do not trod, and wickedness finds no foothold (e.g., Ps. 26:13; 141:6). The parable of the Wicked Tenant recorded in the Gospel of St. Matthew provides a metaphor for both the present and the eschatological fulfillments of the Kingdom of God (Matt. 21-33-43). One can participate in the Kingdom of God as a faithful tenant now while inheriting its fullness as a reward in the future[162].

The virtue of meekness is acquired by imitating the meekness of Christ. There are boundless opportunities in everyday life to assimilate the virtue of meekness. The Apostle Peter described very well the manifestation of meekness in daily life, "not returning evil for evil or reviling for reviling, but on the contrary blessing, knowing that you were called to this, that you may inherit a blessing" (1 Pet. 3:9). Thus, the imitation of the Son of God in receiving the inheritance of blessing promised to the children of God by conquering sin and the passions by meekness is the pathway by which the soul extends beyond its nature to ever greater participation in the Divine Life (cf. Heb. 2:10-16). Blessed Augustin reminds us of the word of the Apostle Paul[163], "Do not be overcome by evil, but overcome evil with good" (Rom. 12:21). When meekness reaches its fullness, union with God is attained. The soul is possessed only by the true good, giving no existence to sin.

St. Gregory of Nyssa said that humility combined with the mourning over sin is the mother of meekness[164]. The

---

[162] Hamm, *The Beatitudes in Context: What Luke and Matthew Meant*, 91-92.

[163] Augustin, "Our Lord's Sermon on the Mount: Book I", in *Nicene and Post-Nicene Fathers*, 4.

[164] St. Gregory of Nyssa, *The Lord's Prayer, The Beatitudes*, 104.

pathway to theosis is by the assimilation of each virtue embodied in the Beatitudes in the ascent to union with God. Acquiring these virtues reflects the personal, ascetic aspect of progressing toward theosis. The blessings promised for each Beatitude express the grace of the Holy Spirit received in progressing toward theosis, through an ever-greater participation in the Divine Life. The Kingdom of God is accessible to the humble and contrite in spirit, the door of which is opened through repentance and the Sacraments of the Church (e.g., Ps. 51:19; Matt. 4:17; 18:1-5; 28:18-20; Mark 16:14-16; Acts 2:38-39; Col. 2:11-15; Rom. 6:3-11). The soul encounters the obstacle of a nature weakened by sin and afflicted with the passions in the pursuit of the true good, a sorrow that is overcome by the comfort of the Holy Spirit. The soul that conquers evil with good finds rest in the very cost of following the meekness of Christ, as the Lord said in Matthew 11:28-29.

Blessed Augustin said that the inheritance of the earth in the third Beatitude signifies the firmness and stability of the perpetual inheritance of the Kingdom of God.[165] Just as the body rests on the earth and is nourished by the food from the earth, the soul of the follower of Christ, by means of a good disposition, rests and is nourished with its own food. This food is to obey the will of the Father by imitating Christ (John 4:31-34), to be voluntary participants in the Reign of God. The very rest and life of the saints is communion with the Holy Trinity through deifying grace.

> The Angel of the Lord shall encamp around those who fear Him, and He will deliver them. Oh, taste and see that the Lord is good; blessed is the man who hopes in Him. Fear the Lord, you His saints,

---

165 Augustin, "Our Lord's Sermon on the Mount: Book I", in *Nicene and Post-Nicene Fathers*, 4.

for there is no want to those who fear Him. Rich men turned poor and went hungry; but those who seek the Lord shall not lack any good thing... But those who wait on the Lord, these shall inherit the earth... But the gentle shall inherit the earth, and they shall delight in the fullness of peace... The Lord knows the way of the blameless, and their inheritance shall be forever... For those who bless him [the righteous] shall inherit the earth, but those who curse him shall be utterly destroyed... The righteous shall inherit the earth and dwell upon it unto ages of ages... Wait on the Lord, and keep His way, and He shall exalt you to inherit the earth (Ps. 33:8-11; 36:9, 11, 18, 22, 29, 34).

Chapter 6:
Blessed Are Those Who Hunger and Thirst for Righteousness

Blessed are those who hunger and thirst for righteousness, for they shall be filled (Matt. 5:6).

Before arriving at the base of Mount Sinai, the Israelites had to advance through several preparatory stages during their desert sojourning following their exodus from Egypt. In terms of their typological fulfillments, these stages showed that the virtuous life had to take root through inner sanctification and instruction in the faith, and a personal working out of the content of that faith by gaining some victory over sin and the passions. The mountain of divine knowledge, however, is steep and difficult to climb. Further progress in the ascent to God requires continual contemplation and purity of body and soul. This was revealed by God when He instructed Moses to charge the people at the base of the mountain to sanctify themselves and purify their outer garments (Exod. 19:10, 14-15). The solemnity of this next stage in the ascent to God is reflected in the charge that the animals were not allowed even to touch the base of the mountain and live (Exod. 19:13).

Arriving at the base of Mount Sinai in the historical episode from Israel's exodus from Egypt provides the prophetic symbol for understanding the Christian's arrival at the fourth Beatitude, the blessed hungering and thirsting for righteousness. This correlation is seen in the correspondence of the fourth Beatitude with the fourth operation of the Holy Spirit in the list of theophanies in Isiah 11:2-3, which descends from the greater energies of the God to the lesser. Thus, hungering and thirsting for righteousness corresponds to the theophany of "might" (Isa. 11:2-3). As explained by Blessed Augustin, righteousness hungered and thirsted for requires labor and fortitude[166]. This virtue is acquired by vehement exertion to detach from carnal things. Sin that is retained with delight at this stage in the journey to God is not abandoned without pain.

The hungering and thirsting of this Beatitude refer to the appetite of the soul. Appetite is blessed for both body and soul since it is the principle cause of strength[167]. Having arrived at this Beatitude by progressing in humility, godly sorrow and meekness, the soul has been purged of the superfluous satiety of sin and the passions. The soul now hungers and thirsts for its natural food[168].

Christ teaches His followers in this Beatitude about the appetite and food for the soul by analogy with the body. An expanded teaching is found in the Gospel of St. John. After ministering all day, the disciples urged Jesus to eat. "But He said to them, 'I have food to eat of which you do not know. My food is to do the will of Him who sent Me, and to finish His work'" (John 4:32, 34). This passage teaches two important principles. First, the soul (and the body) has a natural appetite. Christ, who "was in all points tempted as we are, yet without sin" (Heb. 4:15), did not eliminate in His

---

166   *Ibid.*, 6.

167   St. Gregory of Nyssa, *The Lord's Prayer, The Beatitudes*, 118.

168   *Ibid.*, 117.

(hypostatic) union with human nature the hunger of the body or the soul, as the appetite of both faculties are needed to preserve life[169]. Thus, overcoming temptation does not eliminate hunger from nature, indicating that appetite is not the cause of evil (cf. James 1:14-15). Rather, virtue is the power of the soul to cast aside all unnatural food. For example, St. John Chrysostom says that hunger and thirst are the peculiar properties of covetousness[170]. The power of virtue is to transfer the desire for covetousness to the new object of righteousness, which frees the soul from covetousness. The wicked counsel of the devil spurns what is natural to consume and entices one to convert and ingest what is unnatural. This is the deeper meaning of the devil tempting Christ to turn stone into bread (Matt. 4:3). The man who is concerned about feeding the soul with things it cannot eat is the man who is busy turning stone into bread[171].

The soul has a natural appetite. Furthermore, the food that is natural for the appetite of the soul is the righteousness of God, as the Beatitude teaches. The second important point that one can extract from the passage of the Gospel of John discussed above is that it provides a concrete example of righteousness as food. Jesus said the food for the human soul is to do the will of God. The will of God is that He "desires all men to be saved and come to the knowledge of the truth" (1 Tim. 2:4). St. Gregory of Nyssa, summarizing these passages (John 4:34; 1 Tim. 2:4), says that the blessed one is he who hungers for the

---

169   *Ibid.*, 123.

170   Chrysostom, "Homily XV: Matt. V. 1,2", in *Nicene and Post-Nicene Fathers*, 94.

171   St. Gregory of Nyssa, *The Lord's Prayer, The Beatitudes*, 121-122.

divine will and thirst for the salvation of his own soul[172]. The metaphors of hunger and thirst are both needed to adequately describe the acquisition of virtue. The follower of Christ must partake of righteousness as food with the intense fervor of desire that is represented by thirst. Chromatius says we must seek after righteousness with earnest desire, not with fainthearted energy[173].

The righteous man is the one who is "right with God," the person who lives out the covenant relationship with God and neighbor[174], according to the law of love (cf. 1 John 2:3-9; 5:1-5). The references to righteousness in the Scripture express the synergy between the divine grace of God and human freedom and will. These two un-equal but equally necessary aspects of righteousness are reflected in Isaiah 61, which is a primary source of the Beatitudes from the prophetic word. The righteousness of God is received as a gift (Isa. 61:3). In addition, righteousness is pursued as a human task, enabled by the saving righteousness of God (Isa. 61:8). These two aspects are also expressed in the occurrences of the word "righteous" in the Gospel of St. Matthew[175]. The occurrence of "righteousness" in the fourth Beatitude expresses both aspects at once with

---

172 *Ibid.,* 124.

173 Chromatius, *Ancient Christian Commentary on Scripture: New Testament Ia; Matthew 1-13,* 84.

174 Hamm, *The Beatitudes in Context: What Luke and Matthew Meant,* 92.

175 *Ibid.,* 93-95. The references in the Gospel of Matthew that reflect the demand and human pursuit of righteousness are the following: doing the will of God (Matt. 3:15; 5:20), practices of piety (Matt. 6:1), and repentance expressed in action (Matt. 21:32). The passages that indicate righteousness as a gift of God are Matthew 5:6 and 6:33. However, the opinion of the author of this book differs with Hamm in that the last two passages express both the gift and the demand at once with an apophatic disposition. The author of this

apophatic emphasis. This Beatitude directs the soul to seek the gift of a right relationship with God. As the Church Fathers says, to hunger and thirst for righteousness is to desire God's own righteousness[176].

From the discussion above, righteousness is not one virtue, or even several virtues. Every virtue is comprised under the righteousness hungered and thirsted for in the fourth Beatitude. The only true and solid food for the soul is the zeal for virtue[177]. It is the fervent hunger and thirst for the soul's true food that will enable the follower of Christ to starve the daily passions and desires of the sinful nature, while at the same time restoring the weakened soul to health by gaining strength through zeal and acquisition of virtue (cf. Heb. 12:3-13).

Virtue is both the work and the reward, as the Beatitude proclaims. The desire for virtue is followed by the possession of it[178]. The interior goodness of acquired virtue brings unceasing joy, as the possession of virtue is to possess the Holy Trinity within oneself. For Christ Jesus is the natural desire and reward of the appetite of the soul. Christ became wisdom from God, justification, sanctification, and redemption[179]. Christ became the living bread and water (John 4:13-15; 6:35) for the soul that thirsts for God (Ps. 41:3). The glory of the Lord will satisfy that soul that seeks the righteousness of God (Ps. 16:15). The one who has tasted of the Lord is truly blessed (Ps. 33:9), as the Psalmist said, because He has been filled with the One

---

book also has the same opinion concerning Matthew 5:10, the eighth Beatitude, which Hamm says stresses the demand only.

176   Anonymous, *Ancient Christian Commentary on Scripture: New Testament Ia; Matthew 1-13*, 84.

177   St. Gregory of Nyssa, *The Lord's Prayer, The Beatitudes*, 126.

178   *Ibid.*, 128.

179   *Ibid.*, 128-129.

whom he has desired. "If anyone loves Me, he will keep My word, and My Father will love him, and We will come in to him and make Our home with him" (John 14:23), along with the Holy Spirit who is already there[180] (John 14:15-17).

The Apostle Paul knew that he possessed what He desired. He said, "I suffer the loss of all things, and count them as rubbish, that I may gain Christ and be found in Him" (Phil. 3:8-9). He also said, "Christ lives in me" (Gal. 2:20). The apostle is filled with what he has desired, yet he is still hungry. This is the apophatic way which leads to theosis. Stretching forth beyond his nature to greater participation in the Divine Life that is set before him, the Apostle Paul said,

> Not that I have already attained, or am already perfected; but I press on, that I may lay hold of that for which Christ Jesus has also laid hold of me. Brethren, I do not count myself to have apprehended; but one thing I do, forgetting those things which are behind and reaching forward to those things which are ahead, I press toward the goal for the prize of the upward call of God in Christ Jesus (Phil. 3:12-14).

The assimilation of virtue, once firmly established, is neither limited by time nor by satiety[181]. It is an eternal growth in the desire and possession of the goodness of God. Jesus promises in the Beatitude that those who hunger and thirst after God will be filled. And having been filled does not dull the desire for ever-greater participation in the Life of the Holy Trinity, but rather brings an ever-fresh

---

180   *Ibid.*, 129.

181   *Ibid.*, 127.

experience of the fullness of the natural delights of the soul, which is God Himself.

> The poor shall eat and be well-filled, and those who seek Him will praise the Lord; their hearts will live unto ages of ages… For the kingdom is the Lord's; and He is the Master of the Gentiles. All the prosperous of the earth ate and worshipped; all going down into the earth shall bow down before Him. And my soul lives with Him. And my seed shall serve Him; the coming generation shall be told of the Lord, and they shall declare His righteousness to a people who will be born, because the Lord made them (Ps. 21:27, 29-32).

Chapter 7:
Blessed Are the Merciful

> Blessed are the merciful, for they shall obtain mercy (Matt. 5:7).

The Beatitudes support one another and prepare the believer to approach God Himself[182]. The believer draws near to God by progressing step-by-step to this Beatitude, as noted by the exhortation of St. James in his epistle (James 4:7-10). Jacob learned that one cannot be raised to God except by always tending to the things above (Gen. 28:10-19; cf. Col. 3:1-4). Theosis is achieved by an unceasing desire for higher things. The apophatic disposition is to count it as loss if one fails to progress further, always stretching toward union with God (cf. Phil. 3:7-11). The Apostle Paul said, "Earnestly desire the best gifts" (1 Cor. 12:31). At this stage, the sojourner has acquired a healthy appetite for virtue, has gained some strength, and has advanced along the pathway to theosis. Having now ascended above the base of the mystical mountain of divine knowledge, in reference to Moses's ascent of Mount Sinai, the fifth Beatitude elevates the follower of Christ to higher contemplation and perceptions of the Divine Life. The Beatitude of mercy is an invitation to become like God, for "the Lord is merciful and righteous, and our God has mercy" (Ps. 114:5).

---

182 *Ibid.*, 130.

The Beatitude of mercy corresponds to "counsel" in the third operation of the Holy Spirit in Isaiah 11:2-3 – i.e., in the list of the seven-fold operation of the Holy Spirit in the descending latter of theophanies. Mercy is associated with "counsel", as Blessed Augustin stated, because mercy is the remedy for escaping the evils of the fallen world[183]. Thus, Jesus counseled His disciples in the Lord's Prayer that they forgive as they wish themselves to be forgiven (Matt. 6:12). The one thing needful for the sinful soul is the mercy of God (Matt. 9:9-13; 12:1-14; cf. Isa. 1:14-20). In the Septuagint OT, and in the NT, the occurrences of the Greek word translated "mercy" are overwhelmingly used as a quality of God[184]. Therefore, if the follower of Christ is merciful, he is deemed worthy of the Divine Beatitude because he has attained to that which characterizes God Himself[185].

St. Gregory of Nyssa provided a beautiful description of the qualities of mercy in his sermons on the Beatitudes[186]. There are the obvious meanings of the word. Mercy is intensified charity that originates in love. It is a loving disposition towards those who suffer distress, a voluntary sorrow that joins itself to the sufferings of others. Mercy transforms both the giver and the receiver of mercy. To the giver of mercy, it softens the soul since it is the opposite of cruelty. The merciful one is predisposed by his attitude to give sympathy. A man cannot heal the ills of his neighbor without it. To the receiver of mercy, it is a maker of friends since it naturally engenders love in those who

---

183 Augustin, "Our Lord's Sermon on the Mount: Book I", in *Nicene and Post-Nicene Fathers*, 6-7.

184 Hamm, *The Beatitudes in Context: What Luke and Matthew Meant*, 92.

185 St. Gregory of Nyssa, *The Lord's Prayer, The Beatitudes*, 131.

186 *Ibid.*, 132-134.

share it. Finally, mercy is the parent of other virtues such as kindness and charity. It is the bond of all loving disposition.

There is another biblical concept of mercy besides extending help to the needy[187], as expressed above (see also Exod. 22:27). The other aspect of mercy is to forgive the guilty (Exod. 34:6-7). An example in the NT of the close connection between mercy and forgiveness is Jesus's Parable of the Unforgiving Servant (Matt. 18:23-35). In this parable, mercy is understood as forgiveness. The background to this parable is the question raised by the Apostle Peter of how many times one should forgive his brother (Matt. 18:21-22). Jesus's answer to Peter is that there is no limit to forgiveness, as mercy and forgiveness characterize the Divine Nature[188]. The logical conclusion of Jesus's parable that followed Peter's question is that the disciple of Christ is able to forgive because he has received forgiveness as a gift from God first. Extending forgiveness to others is imitating Christ and participating in the Divine Life (e.g., Matt. 12:7; Gal. 6:16; Phil. 2:1-2).

Yet mercy is more than these obvious meanings discussed so far, as indicated by the future tense of the reward, "they shall obtain mercy" (Matt. 5:7). The mercy of God is received now (e.g., Matt. 15:22; 17:15; 20:30; 2 Cor. 4:1), but there is also an eschatological dimension[189] with a higher doctrine to be learned[190]. He who is made in the image of God is endowed by his Creator with the principles of all goodness, with the divine gift of the image of God, the potential to become like God through the acquisition

---

187 Hamm, *The Beatitudes in Context: What Luke and Matthew Meant*, 96-98.

188 St. Gregory of Nyssa, *The Lord's Prayer, The Beatitudes*, 131.

189 Hamm, *The Beatitudes in Context: What Luke and Matthew Meant*, 98.

190 St. Gregory of Nyssa, *The Lord's Prayer, The Beatitudes*, 135.

of virtue. Nothing good enters man from outside. Rather, man brings forth the good from his own nature as from some inner chamber. As Jesus said, "the kingdom of God is within you" (Luke 17:21). Furthermore, in the Sermon on the Mount, Jesus said, "everyone who asks receives, and he who seeks finds, and to him who knocks it will be opened" (Matt. 7:8). An aspect of the power of the human will is its capability to attain what it desires. He who truly desires the Kingdom of God will receive it by acquiring virtue, through series of inner purification and contemplation, assisted by the grace of God manifested by the blessed promises of the Beatitudes. Since mercy is an undiminishing property of God, the fifth Beatitude expands the soul by the apophatic approach to advancement in the journey to God.

The apophatic approach to assimilating the virtue of mercy can be explained as follows. Opportunities arise in everyday life to help those in need. Blessed Augustin stated it this way[191]. Out of the fullness of your cup fill an empty person in need, so that your own emptiness may again be filled by the fullness of God. However, these opportunities are limited, and after the Second Coming there will no longer be a need to extend mercy to one's brother (Rev. 21:1-4). The unending mercy in the ascent to union with God is the sympathy and care that one extends to his own soul[192]. In his fallen nature, the spiritual sojourner who has advanced to this stage has pity on his soul because of the sorrowful awareness that it has lost its true beauty. Wrath, hatred, pride, envy, greed, and all vice, are bitter enemies and tyrants of the soul, and have tarnished and disfigured the image of God in each person. In the New Aeon, the soul will still desire its true food, which is communion with the

---

191   Augustine, *Ancient Christian Commentary on Scripture: New Testament Ia; Matthew 1-13*, 85-86.

192   St. Gregory of Nyssa, *The Lord's Prayer, The Beatitudes*, 137.

Holy Trinity. Mercy directed to one's own soul, whether in the fallen world or the age to come, is the movement to supply the soul with its natural need to expand towards greater participation in the Divine Life through the acquisition of virtue. This activity of the soul will surely be reciprocated by Divine Mercy[193]. The fruit of mercy becomes itself the possession of the merciful.

At this stage in the ascent to union with God, the sojourner has been made the friend of God through the blessings of the Beatitudes, since he now possesses that which is properly God's, the beatitude of mercy[194].

> Behold, the eyes of the Lord are on those who fear Him, on those who hope in His mercy, to deliver their souls from death and to keep them alive in famine. Our soul shall wait for the Lord; He is our helper and protector; for our heart shall be glad in Him, and we hope in His holy name. Let your mercy, O Lord, be upon us, as we hope in You (Ps. 32:18-22).

---

193   *Ibid.,* 139.
194   *Ibid.,* 130-131.

Chapter 8:
Blessed Are the Pure in Heart

Blessed are the pure in heart, for they shall see God (Matt. 5:8)

To behold God is the purpose and end of all loving activity, said Blessed Augustin[195]. He continued, "unless your heart be pure, you will not be permitted to see what cannot be seen unless the heart is pure"[196]. In terms of the typologies of Moses's ascent of Mount Sinai discussed in chapter 2, the follower of Christ who has reached the Beatitude of a pure heart has reached the summit of the ascent to God and has entered the inner sanctuary of divine knowledge where God is. St. John Chrysostom said that the pure of heart are those who have attained unto all virtue[197]. Chrysostom calls to mind the words of the apostle: "pursue peace with all people, and holiness, without which no one will see the Lord" (Heb. 12:14). The sixth Beatitude corresponds to the second operation of the seven-fold operation of the Holy Spirit in Isaiah 11:2-3, which is "understanding." This correspondence is understood as follows. According to Blessed Augustin, it

---

195 Augustine, *Ancient Christian Commentary on Scripture: New Testament Ia; Matthew 1-13*, 85-86.

196 Ibid., 86-87.

197 Chrysostom, "Homily XV: Matt. V. 1,2", in *Nicene and Post-Nicene Fathers*, 94.

is from a good conscience of good works that the spiritual sojourner can contemplate the highest good, which is to be discerned from a pure heart[198].

The most obvious OT background for the sixth Beatitude is Psalm 23:3-4: "Who shall ascend the mountain of the Lord? Who shall stand in His holy place? He who has innocent hands and a pure heart." This is an entrance psalm from the vantage point of a worshipper about to enter the Jerusalem temple[199]. The words "innocent" (or "clean") and "purity" are understood in the cultic or ritual sense, which usually refers to time, spaces, persons and things set aside and dedicated to God. However, the psalm also synthesizes the usual meaning of these words with the prophetic tradition which interiorizes ritual language and applies them to the whole of the sojourner's person and life. Thus, the essence of the meaning of this passage is that the one who is fit to "ascend the mountain of the Lord" is the one whose whole life – in external actions, as represented by the hands, and internally, as represented by the heart – is dedicated to God, and therefore, must be "innocent" and "pure".

In the Beatitude, Christ promises that those who have ascended the ladder of virtue will participate in the ineffable and incomprehensible goodness of God, having put on the blessed form. That is, those "who seek the face of the God of Jacob" (Ps. 23:6), will, indeed, "see God", which is made possible by the redemptive work of the Incarnate Christ (cf. Isa. 2:3; 40:9; 2 Cor. 5:14-17). The pure of heart, as Chromatius says, will win the right to see the God of glory[200], no longer "in a mirror, dimly, but then face to face"

---

198   Augustin, "Our Lord's Sermon on the Mount: Book I", in *Nicene and Post-Nicene Fathers*, 6.

199   Hamm, *The Beatitudes in Context: What Luke and Matthew Meant*, 100.

200   Chromatius, *Ancient Christian Commentary on Scripture: New*

(1 Cor. 13:12). Knowing that God can only be seen with a pure heart, King David prays, "create in me a clean heart, O God" (Ps. 50:12). The promise is so great that it transcends the utter limits of beatitude[201]. In Scripture, the use of the phrase "to see" means the same thing as "to have" (Ps. 127:5; Isa. 26:10). The man who sees God possesses in this act of seeing all that is good: life everlasting, eternal incorruption, undiminished beatitude, unconditional happiness and the unceasing enjoyment of the Kingdom of God.

In the aftermath of the soul's exuberance caused by such a marvelous prospect of seeing God, one is led by further reflection to a paradox evident with this Beatitude, on which St. Gregory of Nyssa elaborates so eloquently. On the one hand, God is promised to the vision of those whose heart is purified, for to see the Lord is to know Him and to have eternal life[202]. Moses and the Apostles John and Paul participated in the transcendent Beatitude that consists in seeing God[203]. God said to Moses, "you have found grace in My sight, and I know you above all" (Exod. 33:17). In referring to Jesus, the Apostle John said:

> That which was from the beginning, which we have heard, which we have seen with our eyes, and which we have looked upon, and our hands have handled, concerning the Word of life – the life was manifested and we have seen, and bear witness, and declare to you that eternal life which was with the Father and manifested to us (1 John 1:1-2).

Testament Ia; Matthew 1-13, 87.

201 St. Gregory of Nyssa, *The Lord's Prayer, The Beatitudes*, 144.
202 *Ibid.*, 143.
203 *Ibid.*, 145.

Moreover, the Apostle Paul said, "there is laid up for me the crown of righteousness, which the Lord, the righteous Judge, will give me on that Day" (2 Tim. 4:8).

On the other hand, these same three pillars of the faith explicitly denied all possibility of the apprehension of God[204]. Again, God said to Moses, "you cannot see My face; for no man can see My face and live" (Exod. 33:7). The Apostle John said, "no one has seen God at any time" (John 1:18; 1 John 4:12). Furthermore, in speaking of Christ Jesus, the Apostle Paul said, "He who is the blessed and only Potentate, the King of kings and Lord of lords, who alone has immortality, dwelling in unapproachable light, whom no man has seen or can see, to whom be honor and everlasting power. Amen" (1 Tim. 6:15-16).

The apparent paradox discussed above is resolved by apprehending the two-fold meaning of seeing God. One mode of seeing God is to know the Divine Nature that is above all things (e.g., Ps. 146:5; Dan. 3:52). The saints have declared this mode of knowledge impossible for all created order[205]. The knowledge of Divine Essence is inaccessible[206]. Whatever the Divine Nature is in Itself, it surpasses every concept. It is inaccessible to conjecture and reasoning. There is no human faculty, whether it be reason or perception, capable of apprehending the incomprehensible Divine Nature. The ways of God are unsearchable (Rom. 11:33).

The second mode of seeing God is knowing Him in His divine energies, which leads to union with God through purity of life. The Divinity of the Holy Trinity, according to Pseudo-Dionysius the Areopagite, is fully manifested

---

204   *Ibid.*, 143.
205   *Ibid.*, 151.
206   *Ibid.*, 146.

and entirely present in the energies[207]. God is revealed both in His essence, which is inaccessible to the created order, and in the free acts of His divine energies, which are accessible[208]. The Lord has promised to human nature this form of contemplation in the sixth Beatitude[209], and the saints witness to this mode of seeing God (e.g., Ps. 67:36; 81:6; Eph. 1:15-23; Jude 24-25). This means that the Invisible and Incomprehensible God is seen through participation in the Divine Life and communion with the Holy Trinity.

The apophatic way is the approach to seeing God in His divine energies which leads the believer to union with God[210]. To begin the process, God is seen secondarily by inference through the wisdom that appears in the universe[211] (Ps. 103:24). Moreover, the Goodness of God is apprehended through His revelation in Scripture, for the divine word proclaims that God created the universe not out of necessity, but from the free will of His Goodness (Eph. 1:3-6). Other apprehensions of God from the created order and from Scripture abound: such as His power, purity, immutability, simplicity, humility, mercy, etc. Therefore, God is invisible and incomprehensible by nature, but becomes visible in His divine energies, and can be contemplated in the things that reveal and communicate His Divine Person.

The fullness of the attainment of the sixth Beatitude is not the secondary knowledge of God derived by analogy

---

207 Lossky, *In the Image and Likeness of God*, 41.

208 John Meyendorff, *St. Gegory Palamas and Orthodox Spirituality*, trans. Adele Fiske (Crestwood, NY: St. Vladimir's Press, 1974), 123.

209 St. Gregory of Nyssa, *The Lord's Prayer, The Beatitudes.*, 151.

210 Lossky, *The Mystical Theology of the Eastern Church*, 28, 29.

211 St. Gregory of Nyssa, *The Lord's Prayer, The Beatitude.*, 146-147.

through His divine operations discussed above. That degree of contemplation merely forms the basis for the perfect way of seeing God intended by the promise of Christ in the Beatitude. To see God is to contemplate His personal existence in the theophanies of His manifesting energies, achieved through the imitation of Christ and the gift of the Holy Spirit (Eph. 1:13-14; 2:4-10; 1 Pet. 1:1-3). Pseudo-Dionysius describes this double movement in the following way[212]. First, God reveals Himself in His energies. This is a personal encounter, and the divine will is addressed to the creature. There is a subsequent synergy of two wills, the predetermination of God and the liberty of the creature. Secondly, the creature rises towards theosis, transcending the manifestation of God in His energies. Progress towards deification is the cooperation of the human ascetic work of inner transformation, through purity of life, with the deifying grace of the Holy Spirit (1 Cor. 3:9; Ps:81:6; John 10:34-35; 2 Pet. 1:2-11).

Thus, the apophatic way undergirds the fundamental directive of the Christian life, which is the progressive ascent of following Christ, Who is the "Way" (John 14:6) in the divine ascent towards the source of all manifesting energy[213] – i.e., the ascent towards the monarchy of the Father, which is achieved through union with Christ in the Holy Spirit (e.g., John 14:6, 15-28; 16:5-15; 17:6-26; 1 John 2:20-27). St. Gregory of Nyssa provides an example from human nature that distinguishes the blessedness of the direct[214] knowledge of experience over secondary

---

212   Lossky, *In the Image and Likeness of God*, 41-42.

213   *Ibid.*, 16.

214   Veniamin, *The Orthodox Understanding of Salvation*, 166-167. St. Gregory Palamas affirms that even is the present life of man, direct knowledge of God as the experience of unmediated communion with Him is possible.

knowledge[215]. Bodily health is blessed not because one knows the principles of good health, but because one is, in fact, healthy. Applying this analogy to the knowledge of God, St. Gregory said, "the Lord does not say it is blessed to know something about God, but to have God present within oneself"[216]. The blessedness of seeing God, therefore, is the knowledge of God gained by the experience of communion with the Holy Trinity through participation in the divine energies. Participation in the Divine Life is attained through the synergy of the ascetic struggle to acquire sanctification with the deifying grace of the Holy Spirit (1 Thess. 4:3-8; Titus 2:11-14; 3:4-8).

St. Gregory of Nyssa discusses the nature in which the follower of Christ participates in the Divine Life and is united to God[217]. The key is found in the words of Jesus, "the kingdom of God is within you" (Luke 17:21). The contact between God and man takes place in the inner man, the place of the heart. Man is created in the image of and likeness of God (Gen. 1:26-26). Therefore, the image of God forms the ontological basis of man's union with God. The image is the likeness of the glories of God's own nature imprinted upon human nature. However, this likeness is covered over by the filth of sin. When the dirt and grime of the soul are scraped off, man will recover the likeness of the archtype and be good. The Godhead is purity, freedom from passion, and the separation from all evil. If man's heart is purified from evil and unruly passions, he will see the image of the Divine Nature in his own beauty. St. John Chrysostom said that those who are pure have so filled

---

215 St. Gregory of Nyssa, *The Lord's Prayer, The Beatitudes*, 147-148.

216 *Ibid.*, 148.

217 *Ibid.*, 148-150.

their lives with goodness that they are practically unaware of evil within themselves[218]. Whoever possess goodness possesses God and is united to him.

The vision of God is purity, sanctity, and simplicity. The pure of heart sees what is invisible to those who are not purified because the pure of heart have been cleansed[219]. Thus, the pure of heart sees himself. In seeing himself, he sees the natural desire of human nature. He becomes blessed because when he looks at his own purity, he sees the archtype in the image. And what is like the Good must itself be certainly good. The pure of heart, therefore, have attained to participation in the Divine Life, fulfilling the natural desire of man.

St. Gregory of Nyssa succinctly summarizes the way to acquire purity of heart[220]. Wickedness can be divided up into two categories: thoughts and actions. The Old Law punishes the actions of evils works. The New Law does not abolish the Old Law but perfects it (Matt. 5:19). The New Law removes evil from the very choice of the will, guarding the soul against the very beginning of evil (cf. James 1:14-15). This frees life perfectly from wicked works. In the rest of the Sermon on the Mount, the divine Word by His commands digs up the evil roots in the depths of the human heart as if by a plough. The divine commands purify the heart by purging it from bringing forth thorns. For example, the disease of wrath is cured by purging the heart of anger (Matt. 5:21-26). Sins committed for the sake of pleasure are healed by uprooting lust (Matt. 5:27-32). Unjust violence is abolished by not permitting self-defense

---

218 Chrysostom, *Ancient Christian Commentary on Scripture: New Testament Ia; Matthew 1-13*, 86.

219 St. Gregory of Nyssa, *The Lord's Prayer, The Beatitudes*, 149-150.

220 *Ibid.*, 151-153.

(Matt. 5:38-39). Covetousness in banished by giving up what is left when robbed or taken advantage of (Matt. 5:40-42).

The "understanding" of the Holy Spirit (Isa. 11:1-2) is incarnated by the follower of Christ when each day is seized as a sequence of opportunities to purge the heart of evil desires, "bringing every thought into captivity to the obedience of Christ" (2 Cor. 10:5). For the weapons of this warfare are not carnal but mighty in God. They are the virtuous life and the degree of blessed participation in the Divine Life acquired so far, in advancing along the pathway to theosis through ascending the ladder of the Beatitudes.

> Who shall ascend to the mountain of the Lord? Who shall stand in His holy place? He who has innocent hands and a pure heart; He who does not lift up his soul to vanity; He who does not swear deceitfully to his neighbor. He shall receive blessing from the Lord and mercy from the God of his salvation. This is the generation of those who seek Him, Who seek the face of the God of Jacob (Ps. 23:3-6).

Chapter 9:
Blessed Are the Peacemakers

> Blessed are the peacemakers, for they shall be called sons of God (Matt. 5:9).

The blessedness of seeing God is the fulfillment of the typologies surrounding Moses's ascent to the summit of Mount Sinai and his entrance into the inner sanctuary of divine knowledge where God is, as discussed in the last chapter. When Moses passed on to the "tabernacle not made with human hands" (Heb. 9:11), he perceived the mystery of the Incarnation, the divinity of Christ who pitched His tabernacle among us (John 1:1-5, 14). The blessedness of seeing the glory and goodness of God in Christ, "through whom also He [God] made the worlds; who being the brightness of His glory and the express image of His person, who upholding all things by the word of His power" (Heb. 1:2-3), transcends the limits of beatitude. What spiritual ascent can be achieved beyond the vision of God and the possession of His goodness (Ps. 127:5; Isa. 26:10)? Can the soul ascend any higher in its journey to God? Is there anything beyond the vision of God in the pathway to theosis? The answer is yes, which is affirmed by the seventh Beatitude.

The unfathomable promise of the seventh Beatitude is divine sonship, which is grace that transcends nature[221].

---

221   *Ibid.*, 154, 157.

The blessedness of the seventh Beatitude is participation in the Divine Life that exceeds the experiences of Moses in the Sinai desert. Moses radiated the glory of God (Exod. 34:29-35); yet, it was a glory that eventually faded away (2 Cor. 3:7-8). The one who has received the grace of adoption as a son is alive in the Spirit, no longer a slave to sin and the passions, and has been made a brother of Christ and an heir of God (Luke 20:34-36; Rom. 8:13-17; 9:26; Gal. 4:4-7; Heb. 2:10-13).

St. Gregory of Nyssa characterized the promise of the seventh Beatitude in the following way[222]. In his fallen, creaturely state, man is esteemed as nothing. Abraham described man as dust and ashes (Gen. 18:27). The prophets say that man is grass (Isa. 40:6; Ps. 36:2), and the wisdom tradition ascribes vanity to man (Eccles. 1:2). In addition, the Apostle Paul confesses his own miserable state (1 Cor. 15:9). Nevertheless, the redemptive work of Jesus Christ through the Holy Spirit elevates the follower of Christ to kinship with Almighty God the Father, who can be neither seen nor heard nor thought (Isa. 40:12, 18, 25; 46:5; Eccles. 5:1). Therefore, man is received as a son of God, transcending his own nature, "a god from man" according to St. Gregory[223] and affirmed by Scripture (Ps. 81:6; John 10:34-35).

Through God's love of man, He brings human nature, dishonored by sin, to an honor that almost equals His own[224], through the redemptive work of Christ in the Spirit. If man is made worthy of becoming a son of God, he will possess in himself the dignity of the Father and be made heir of the Father's goods. The Apostle Paul put it this way:

---

222   *Ibid.*, 154-156.

223   *Ibid.*, 156.

224   *Ibid.*, 156.

> But we speak the wisdom of God in a mystery, the hidden wisdom which God ordained before the ages for our glory, which none of the rulers of this age knew; for had they known, they would not have crucified the Lord of glory. But it is written: "Eye has not seen, nor ear heard, nor have entered into the heart of man the things which God has prepared for those who love Him." But God has revealed them to us through His Spirit. For the Spirit searches all things, yes, the deep things of God... Now we have received, not the spirit of the world, but the Spirit who is from God, that we might know the things that have been freely given to us by God... Do you not know that you are the temple of God and that the Spirit of God dwells in you?...Therefore let no one boast in men. For all things are yours: whether Paul or Apollos or Cephas, or the world or life or death, or things present or things to come – all are yours. And you are Christ's, and Christ is God's... the mystery which has been hidden from ages and generations, but now has been revealed to His saints. To them God willed to make known what are the riches of the glory of this mystery among the Gentiles: which is Christ in you, the hope of glory. (1 Cor. 2:7-10, 12; 3:16, 21-23; Col. 1:26-27).

Thus, the seventh Beatitude corresponds to the first and highest of the seven-fold operations of the Holy Spirit in Isaiah 11:2-3, which is "wisdom." This is evident from the Apostle Paul's epistles quoted above. This hidden wisdom of God has been revealed by Jesus Christ through the Holy Spirit. Christ shines forth the glory and radiance of the Goodness of God in His love toward man, revealing the mystery of the divine purpose of man, the divine call and the gift of sonship, making straight the pathway for man to obtain the inheritance of the Kingdom of God and his rightful place at the right hand of Almighty God the Father (Eph. 1:3-6; Col. 3:1-4; Heb. 1:1-4; 12:1-2). These "exceedingly great and precious promises" (2 Pet. 1:4) belong to the peacemakers. It is the peacemakers who have been crowned with the grace of adopted sons[225]. The peacemaker, said Blessed Augustin, has been reformed after the image of God by means of regeneration of the new man, and has acquired the likeness of God, being perfectly wise[226]. The peacemaker has reached the contemplation of the truth through the series of inner purification required to ascend the ladder of Beatitudes and acquire their virtues, tranquillizing the whole man such that all things have been brought into order, and no passion is in a state of rebellion against the truth[227].

The Hebrew word for peace, *shalom*, and its usual Greek counterpart in the OT Septuagint, means far more than the absence of war. The scriptural concept of peace entails a fullness of life, abundance, and right relationships all around[228]. St. Gregory of Nyssa provided a description of the characteristics of peace in his sermons on the Beatitudes[229]. According to St. Gregory, peace is a loving disposition towards one's neighbor. Furthermore, peace is opposed to anything that is opposite of love. Examples

---

225 *Ibid.*, 157.

226 Augustin, "Our Lord's Sermon on the Mount: Book I", in *Nicene and Post-Nicene Fathers*, 6-7.

227 *Ibid.*, 6.

228 Hamm, *The Beatitudes in Context: What Luke and Matthew Meant*, 102.

229 St. Gregory of Nyssa, *The Lord's Prayer, The Beatitudes*, 159.

are anger and wrath[230], envy and hypocrisy[231]. The inner workings of envy and hypocrisy are worse diseases of the soul than the outer expressions of anger and wrath, since a hidden evil is more dangerous than an obvious one. This is clear from the transgression of Cain. The envy Cain had over the praise Abel received from God commanded the murder. But hypocrisy became the executioner, as Cain under the guise of friendship led Abel into the field and away from his parent's help to reveal the murder.

There is no noun or adjective in the OT that one would translate "peacemaker". Jesus uses this word, according to St. Gregory of Nyssa, to convey that God wants every Christian to have peace in such measure as to not keep it only for himself, but to be able to distribute from the overflow of his abundance to others. Thus, the peacemaker gives peace to another[232].

Analogous to the development of the previous Beatitudes, the virtue of peacemaker is acquired through the grace of the Holy Spirit and by imitating the peacemaking work of Christ. One of the most powerful OT images of peacemaking is recorded by the prophet Isaiah[233], a passage which provided the very context, foundation and purpose of the Beatitudes, as discussed in the introduction chapter:

> Now it shall come to pass in the last days, the mountain of the Lord and the house of God shall be visible on the tops of the mountains and exalted above the hills. All the Gentiles shall come to it.

---

230 *Ibid.*, 159-162.

231 *Ibid.*, 162-164.

232 *Ibid.*, 158-159.

233 Hamm, *The Beatitudes in Context: What Luke and Matthew Meant*, 102-103.

> Many Gentiles shall travel and say, "Come and let us go up the mountain of the Lord, to the house of the God of Jacob. He will proclaim His way to us, and we shall walk in it." For the law of the Lord shall go forth from Zion, and the word of the Lord from Jerusalem. He shall judge between the Gentiles and rebuke many people. They shall beat their swords into plows and their spears into pruning hooks. Nation shall not lift up sword against nation, neither shall they learn war anymore (Isa. 2:2-4).

Thus, it is Jesus the Christ who is doing the peacemaking. St. Matthew the Evangelist presents the peacemaking work of Christ by applying the First Servant Song of Isaiah (Isa. 42:1-4) to Jesus's healing of the man with a withered hand on the Sabbath (Matt. 12:9-21). In this passage, St. Matthew presents the Messianic mission of *shalom* as healing and justice applied with gentleness and meekness[234]. The paradox of Jesus's triumphal entry into Jerusalem was already discussed in the chapter on the Beatitude of meekness, where Jesus's humble and peaceful entry was contrasted to King David's violent entry into Jerusalem a millennium earlier. The climax of Christ's peacemaking work is the peace He made by suffering violence from others during His Passion and Crucifixion[235]. Only after His Crucifixion and Resurrection does Christ exercise dominion (Ps. 81:7-8; Zech. 9:10; Matt. 28:18-20; Heb. 12:2).

The sons of God participate in the Father's peacemaking work in Christ through the Holy Spirit[236]. Divine sonship

---

234 *Ibid.*, 104-105.
235 *Ibid.*, 105.
236 Ibid., 105-106.

is both a gift and a work. Participation in Jesus's obedient sonship is through the imitation of His love[237]. St. John Chrysostom said that the peacemaking work of Christ is to unite the divided and reconcile the alienated[238]. As the theanthropic Body of Christ, the peacemaking mission of the Church is the task of discipling the nations (Matt. 28:18-20). In broad terms, the peacemaking work of each member of the Body of Christ is to love one's enemies (Matt. 5:43-48). The Apostle Paul expounded upon the theme of peacemaking through imitation of the love of Christ:

> Repay no one evil for evil. Have regard for good things in the sight of all men. If it is possible, as much as depends on you, live peaceably with all men. Beloved, do not avenge yourself, but rather give place to wrath: for it is written, "Vengeance is Mine, I will repay," says the Lord. Therefore, "If your enemy is hungry, feed him; if he is thirsty, give him a drink; for in doing so you will heap coals of fire on his head." Do not be overcome by evil, but overcome evil with good (Rom. 12:17-21).

The children of God are also peacemakers in themselves, as explained by Blessed Augustin[239]. The peacemakers bring all the motions of the soul into order, such that carnal lusts are thoroughly subdued, becoming a Kingdom of God within (cf. Luke 17:21). It is from this inner reign of the Kingdom of God, brought to a condition of thorough

---

237   *Ibid.*, 104.

238   Chrysostom, "Homily XV: Matt. V. 1,2", in *Nicene and Post-Nicene Fathers*, 94-95.

239   Augustin, "Our Lord's Sermon on the Mount: Book I", in *Nicene and Post-Nicene Fathers*, 6-7.

peace and order, that the prince of this world is cast out, for the devil rules where there is perversity and disorder. The persecutions of the devil now occur from without. This state of inward peace increases the glory of God since the great strength which has been built from within outwardly is made known.

The peacemaker has reached the perfection of the imitation of Christ. St. Gregory of Nyssa says that, as a son of God, the peacemaker imitates the Divine love of men. The peacemaker shines forth in his own life the characteristics of divine energy[240]. The Lord and Giver of good things annihilates completely anything that is foreign to goodness. This work is ordained for the sons of God: to cast out hatred and abolish war, to exterminate envy and strife, to eradicate hypocrisy and extinguish resentment. As light follows darkness, these evil things are replaced by the fruits of the Spirit (Gal. 5:22-23). He who banishes the evil of human nature and introduces a share of the good performs the work of Divine power. For this reason, Christ calls the peacemaker a son of God, because he imitates the true God.

The perfected state of the peacemaker is also well characterized by St. Gregory of Nyssa. The peacemaker goes beyond the two-fold composition of flesh and spirit in man[241]. The peacemaker eliminates the discord between flesh and spirit and the war inherent in human nature (Rom. 7:14-25). The law of the body is no longer at war with the law of the spirit, but subject to the divine command. The peacemaker returns to the good, becomes simple and free from deceit. The peacemaker is truly one: what appears on the outside is the same as what is hidden,

---

240   St. Gregory of Nyssa, *The Lord's Prayer, The Beatitudes*, 164.

241   *Ibid.*, 165.

and what is hidden is the same as what appears. In this state, the Beatitude has come true, for such men are called the sons of God.

The peacemaker has attained theosis, a union with God that knows no limit, but eternally progresses in ever-greater participation in the Divine Life and communion with the Holy Trinity. Moses received the gift of divine illumination at the summit of Mount Sinai and perceived the mystery of the Incarnation, the "tabernacle not made with human hands" (Heb. 9:11). However, the blessing of the grace of adoption as sons of God is incomparably greater than the glory experienced by Moses. Divine sonship is grace that transfigures nature. The soul of the peacemaker has become the Holy of Holies, by entering the Divine Life of the Holy Trinity through the flesh of Jesus Christ, the Offering and the High Priest, and the sanctifying and deifying work of the Holy Spirit (cf. 1 Cor. 1:30; 2:7-12; 3:21-23; Heb. 10:19-25; 1 Pet. 1:1-2). It is within the hidden depths of man's heart that the inaccessible, transcendent God dwells (Ps. 41:8), as a source of divine riches, always seeking to incarnate His Presence[242] (John 15:1-5). The sons of God have become "partakers of the divine nature, having escaped the corruption that is in the world through lust" (2 Pet. 1:4).

> Who is the man who desires life, who loves to see good days? Keep your tongue from evil, and your lips from speaking deceit. Shun evil and do good; seek peace and pursue it (Ps. 33:13-15).

---

242 Metropolitan Philip (Saliba) and Joseph Allen, *Meeting the Incarnate God: From the Human Depths to the Mystery of Fidelity*, 8.

Chapter 10: Participation in the Eighth Day

> Blessed are those who are persecuted for righteousness' sake, for theirs is the kingdom of heaven (Matt. 5:10).

Blessed Augustin says that the first seven Beatitudes bring the follower of Christ to perfection, while the eighth one returns to the starting point, as evident by the reward of the eighth Beatitude expressed in the same terms as the first[243]. St. John Chrysostom notes that Jesus used various names for the rewards of the previous Beatitudes (comfort, inheritance, satisfaction, mercy, vision of God, and divine sonship), yet He brings all those who have obtained these rewards into His kingdom. Thus, the previous rewards are a shadow of the Kingdom, and those who enjoy these rewards will surely attain unto the Kingdom of God[244].

The eighth Beatitude reveals and commends what is complete by bringing into light what is perfect, according to Blessed Augustin[245]. The Kingdom of God within (Luke

---

243 Augustin, "Our Lord's Sermon on the Mount: Book I", in *Nicene and Post-Nicene Fathers*, 6.

244 Chrysostom, "Homily XV: Matt. V. 1,2", in *Nicene and Post-Nicene Fathers*, 95.

245 Augustin, "Our Lord's Sermon on the Mount: Book I", in *Nicene and Post-Nicene Fathers*, 6-7.

17:21) has been perfected by the previous stages of spiritual progress expressed by the first seven Beatitudes. The eighth Beatitude makes manifest the perfect man.

The symbolism of the eighth day in Scripture and Jewish apocalypticism figured prominently in the Church Father's interpretation of the eighth Beatitude. St. Gregory of Nyssa notes that the mystery of the number eight appears as superscripts of Psalms 6 and 11. The Psalmist signifies the Day of Resurrection through the mystery of the eighth day[246]. The eighth day is the time of the history of salvation, which is founded in the eschatological realization of the Day of the Messiah[247].

The symbolism of the eighth day appears elsewhere in Scripture. In the OT, circumcision, which means casting away of the dead skins, occurred on the eighth day. Circumcision was the means of initiation into the community of God's people (Gen. 17:10-14). The deeper meaning of circumcision, provided by the Gospel, is the purification obtained from man's return from defilement to his natural purity[248], an initiation rite that is now replaced by the sacrament of baptism in the community of the New Israel inaugurated by Jesus Christ (Matt. 28:18-20; Mark 16:15-16; Acts 2:38-39; Gal. 3:26-29; Col. 2:11-15). St. Basil the Great draws on the Jewish and Christian interpretations of the eighth day mentioned by the Psalmist (Ps. 6 and 11) to discern that the characteristics and promise of the eternity of the New Aeon are even revealed in the beginning passages of the creation account in the Book of Genesis[249].

---

246 St. Gregory of Nyssa, *The Lord's Prayer, The Beatitudes*, 166.

247 Alexander Schmemann, *Introduction to Liturgical Theology*, trans. Ashleigh E. Moorehouse (Crestwood, NY: St. Vladimir's Press, 1966), 77.

248 St. Gregory of Nyssa, *The Lord's Prayer, The Beatitudes*, 166.

249 Basil the Great, "The Hexaemeron", in *Nicene and Post-Nicene*

Moreover, the risen Jesus appeared to His disciples on the eighth day (John 20:26). Thus, the fallen world and the limits of the old aeon are overcome by the advent of the Lord's Day[250]. Thus, the Eighth Day is the day beyond the limits of the created order. It is the first day of the New Aeon, the time of the Messiah. The eighth day was also interpreted in the Book of Enock as the beginning of the New Aeon not to be reckoned with time[251].

In addition, the eighth day became the day of the Eucharist in which the Church confesses the Resurrection of Christ and participates the Divine Life. In early Christianity, up to the time of St. Basil the Great, the day of the Eucharist was often called the Eighth Day[252]. The symbolism of the eighth day was adopted by the Church and became one of the theological *keys* to its liturgical consciousness, and a prophetic symbol for the breaking-in of the New Aeon in ordinary time by participation in the Life of the Risen Lord.

Considering the discussion above, the eighth Beatitude is the re-instatement in heaven of those who had fallen into servitude to sin and the passions and are now delivered from their slavery into participation in the Kingdom of God[253]. In the eighth Beatitude, the spiritual sojourner returns to the starting point in the ascent to union with God, which is both the beginning and the destiny of the pathway to theosis. The starting point is the day of Pentecost when the Holy Spirit was sent, and by Whom the

---

Fathers. Vol. 8. Basil: Letters and Selected Works; Second Series, eds. Philip Schaff and Henry Wave, 5th printing (Peabody, MA: Hendrickson, 2012), 64-65.

250   Schmemann, *Introduction to Liturgical Theology*, 77.

251   *Ibid.*, 77-78.

252   *Ibid.*, 78.

253   St. Gregory of Nyssa, *The Lord's Prayer, The Beatitudes*, 166.

follower of Christ is led into the Kingdom of God, which is also the destiny. And having been perfected in assimilating the previous Beatitudes, the son of God is able to bear all the troubles brought upon him from without for the sake of truth and righteousness[254].

St. John Chrysostom expounds upon what is persecuted for righteousness' sake[255]. According to St. John, righteousness is the whole practical wisdom of the soul. Therefore, to be persecuted for righteousness' sake is to be persecuted for virtues' sake, for relief given to others, and for godliness. It is not possible for one unarmed by the virtues to go forth unto conflicts of persecution and reviling (Matt. 5:10-11). As a result, the Beatitudes form a golden chain for which the follower of Christ ascends to the perfection of virtue. He who is humble will mourn for his sins; he who mourns will be meek and righteous and merciful. He who possesses these virtues will be pure in heart and a peacemaker. He who has attained these virtues will be arrayed against dangers to body and soul, and will not be troubled by evil, and able to endure trials with patience (cf. James 1:2-4).

The blessing of the persecuted and reviled (Matt. 5:10-12), as explained by St. John Chrysostom, is not in their escaping from affliction, but in their noble endurance of it[256]. He uses the following example from the sensible realm: it is far greater to be struck and not hurt than to escape the blow altogether. The Apostle Paul also proclaims triumph to those who are reviled and endure reproaches (Heb. 10:32-33).

---

254 Augustin, "Our Lord's Sermon on the Mount: Book I", in *Nicene and Post-Nicene Fathers*, 7.

255 Chrysostom, "Homily XV: Matt. V. 1,2", in *Nicene and Post-Nicene Fathers*, 95.

256 *Ibid.*, 96.

Sts. John Chrysostom and Gregory of Nyssa provide descriptions of the nature of the afflictions endured by the persecuted in the eighth Beatitude. One naturally thinks of the prophets and martyrs of the faith who suffered torture and death and other calamities for their testimony (e.g., Heb. 11:4-28). This is certainly true, but the saints who suffered bodily do not include all the persecuted and reviled represented by the eighth Beatitude. Not everyone in the Body of Christ will suffer physically and receive a martyr's death. On the other hand, everyone who has been brought to perfection and has received the blessing of entrance and participation in the Kingdom of God will endure trials and afflictions. St. John Chrysostom offers the example of Job, who was disturbed in his soul when his friends ascribed his afflictions to the penalty for some unseen and unconfessed wickedness of his own[257]. King David also had a similar struggle with those who cursed him (2 Sam. 16:11-12).

Thus, it is true from the previous examples that men's evil reports can have a sharper bite than their evil deeds. The blessed one who endures these types of trials with endurance does not fear reproaches on earth, but desires what is in heaven[258]. One who rejoices in the praise of others and how much they praise him is saddened when he receives no praise. A person who is not lifted up by other's praise is not lowered by their reproach. One who constantly seeks glory on earth constantly fears trouble on earth. But the person who seeks glory only from God fears no disturbance except for God's judgement.

St. Gregory of Nyssa used the patriarch Joseph as an example of one who received blessing for enduring

---

257 Ibid., 96.

258 Anonymous, *Ancient Christian Commentary on Scripture: New Testament Ia; Matthew 1-13*, 91.

persecution[259]. At some point in life, everyone can identify with Joseph, knowing how hard it is to bear people who scheme against us instead of loving us. Through being betrayed and sold into slavery, Joseph became the king of those who had planned evil against him. Joseph would likely not have attained such great dignity had not his brother's envy paved the way for him to inherit the kingdom. It would have been hard for Joseph to think it possible for such an evil purpose to become the source of happiness and bring about a good end. But it did (Gen. 45:4-8). Therefore, the Lord presents beforehand the goal of the struggle in the eighth Beatitude, so that the follower of Christ may more easily overcome the transitory feelings of afflictions[260].

The blessed one who has received the inheritance of the Kingdom God has made his soul ready and capable of receiving the gift of the Kingdom through perfection in the virtuous life, by assimilating the previous Beatitudes through the deifying grace of the Holy Spirit. The eighth Beatitude emphasizes that the one who has attained theosis has used the persecutor (fallen nature and the devil) to help him attain the Good. Being pursued by evil becomes the cause of attaining the good. Human life lies between the boundaries of good and evil. The one who has abandoned the transcendent Good has sunk into the pit of destruction, while he who becomes a total stranger to the corruption of sin approaches the incorruptible Divine Life of the Holy Trinity. This is how we understand persecution for righteousness' sake as being blessed[261]. The apostle said:

---

259 St. Gregory of Nyssa, *The Lord's Prayer, The Beatitudes*, 169.
260 *Ibid.*, 169-170.
261 *Ibid.*, 168-169.

> If you endure chastening, God deals with you as with sons; for what son is there whom a father does not chasten? But if you are without chastening, of which all have become partakers, then you are illegitimate and not sons. Furthermore, we have had human fathers who corrected us, and paid them respect. Shall we not much more readily be in subjection to the Father of spirits and live? For they indeed for a few days chastened us as seemed best to them, but He for our profit, that we may be partakers of His holiness. Now no chastening seems to be joyful for the present, but painful: nevertheless, afterward it yields the peaceable fruit of righteousness to those who have been trained by it. Therefore, strengthen the hands which hang down, and the feeble knees, and make straight paths for your feet, so that what is lame may not be dislocated, but rather be healed (Heb. 12:7-13).

As a result, St. Gregory of Nyssa deduced that the Lord may just have well said in the eighth Beatitude: Blessed are those who are separated from disease for my sake[262]. In other words, blessed is the man who is driven away from all that is hostile, from corruption, darkness, and sin, from injustice and covetousness, from anything that is not virtuous, whether in words, deeds, or thoughts. To be separated from evil means to be confirmed in goodness (John 8:34). If a man is released from these things, he lives in the Kingdom of God. For the rational nature lives in one of two elements of the created universe – either in heaven or on earth. If one is not chased away from earth, he lives

---

262 *Ibid.*, 173.

on earth; but if one departs from the earth, he is translated to heaven[263].

St. Gregory of Nyssa concluded his sermon on the eighth Beatitude with the following exhortation[264]. Let us be persecuted so that we may run. But if we run, let us not run in vain. Let us race towards the prize of our upward vocation (1 Cor. 9:24), which is theosis (Ps. 81:6; John 10:34-35; 2 Pet. 1:4). The pathway to theosis is to ascend the ladder of the Beatitudes through the deifying grace of the Holy Spirit, assimilating the Beatitudes through the series of inner purification and contemplation, and by imitating the Life of Jesus Christ our God our Savior and our Lord. Sharing in the life, afflictions and persecutions of our Lord can only mean sharing in His vindication (Matt. 26:26-29; Luke 22:14-20, 28-30; Rom. 6:3-11; Col. 2:11-15; 3:1-11; Gal. 2:20; 3:26-29; 4:6-7). In the words of the Apostle Paul, "The Spirit Himself bears witness with our spirit that we are children of God, and if children, then heirs – heirs of God and joint heirs with Christ, if we indeed suffer with Him, that we may also be glorified together" (Rom. 8:16-17).

> For the End, concerning the eighth; a psalm of David. Save me, O Lord, for the holy man has ceased; the truthful are diminished from among the sons of men. Each one speaks useless things to his neighbor; deceptive lips speak with a double heart. May the Lord destroy all deceptive lips and the tongue that speaks boastful things, saying, "We will make our tongue powerful; our lips are our own; who is Lord over us?" "Because of the

---

263   *Ibid.*, 173-174.
264   *Ibid.*, 174.

suffering of the needy and because of the groaning of the poor, now I will arise," says the Lord; "I will establish them in salvation; I will declare it boldly." The words of the Lord are pure words, like silver fired in a furnace of earth, purified seven times. You shall guard us, O Lord; you shall preserve us from this generation forever. The ungodly walk in a circle; in Your exaltation, You highly exalted the sons of men (Ps. 11).

Epilogue

When Moses desired to attain to participation in the Divine Life beyond his nature, God told Moses to follow Him from within the cleft of the Rock. The earnest hope of Moses, and all who desire communion with God, was fulfilled through the Incarnation of Jesus Christ, His preaching and healing ministry, His Passion, Death and Crucifixion, His Third-Day Resurrection and Ascension into Heaven, His sitting down at the right hand of God the Father in Heaven, and His sending forth the Holy Spirit at Pentecost. By following the pathway to theosis, imitating the Life of Jesus Christ in ascending the ladder of the Beatitudes through the deifying grace of the Holy Spirit, the darkness of Mount Sinai is transfigured into the light of Mount Tabor[265]. Moses, and all who place their faith and hope in Christ, are at last able to see the glorious face of God incarnate and participate in the Uncreated Light of the Holy Trinity.

> Now after six days Jesus took Peter, James, and John his brother, led them up on a high mountain by themselves; and He was transfigured before them. His face shown like the sun, and His clothes became as white as the light. And behold, Moses and Elijah appeared to them, talking with Him... Now as they came down from the mountain, Jesus commanded them, saying, "Tell the vision to no

---

265 Lossky, *In the Image and Likeness of God*, 43.

one until the Son of Man is risen from the dead" (Matt. 17:1-3, 9).

The Transfiguration is a revelation of the true stature of human nature, the deification of those purified and imbued with spiritual wisdom[266]. Because of the transfiguration of the Divine Word within them, the deified man reflects "with unveiled face, beholding as in a mirror, the glory of the Lord" (2 Cor. 3:18). To see the Transfiguration is to see the Kingdom of God[267]. The Transfiguration also communicates the ecclesial dimension of theosis, as the mystical experience of God is a shared experience, not the propriety of isolated individuals (2 Pet. 1:19-21). Jesus's instruction to His disciples not to tell anyone of the vision until after He had risen from the dead indicates that the glory of the Transfiguration is attained only through the self-emptying of the Passion[268]. The follower of Christ arrives at his true stature of sharing in the glory of Christ by first sharing in the Passion of Christ (Luke 9:23).

The personal, ascetic struggle of sharing in the Passion of Christ is to ascend the ladder of virtues expressed by the Beatitudes. By advancing in the acquisition of virtue, the follower of Christ participates in ever-greater measure in the blessedness of the Divine Life. The eternal progress in the journey of the soul to theosis is marked by deeper communion with God, encountering the ultimate reality behind all goodness in the world, and possessing that

---

266   Russell, *Fellow Workers with God: Orthodox Thinking on Theosis*, 109, 112. In my usage of this reference, I incorporated a partial paraphrase of St. Maximus the Confessor, who sees the Transfiguration as a prefiguration of the Eighth Day, the second and glorious advent of our Lord Jesus Christ.

267   *Ibid.*, 111-112.

268   *Ibid.*, 110.

Goodness within oneself in ever-greater measure. St. John the Evangelist succinctly describes the Beatific Vision:

> Behold what manner of love the Father has bestowed on us, that we should be called children of God! Therefore, the world does not know us, because it did not know Him. Beloved, now we are children of God; and it has not yet been revealed what we shall be, but we know that when His is revealed, we shall see Him as He is. And everyone who has this hope in Him purifies himself, just as He is pure (1 John 3:1-3).

Bibliography

Alfeyev, Metropolitan Hilarion. *Orthodox Christianity Volume II: Doctrine and Teaching of the Orthodox Church*. Translated by Andrew Smith. Yonkers, NY: St. Vladimir's Press, 2012.

Anonymous. *Ancient Christian Commentary on Scripture: New Testament Ia; Matthew 1-13*. Edited by Manlio Simonetti. Downers Grove, IL: InterVarsity Press, 2001.

Augustin. "Our Lord's Sermon on the Mount: Book I." In *Nicene and Post-Nicene Fathers. Vol. 6. Augustin: Sermon on the Mount, Harmony of the Gospels, Homilies on the Gospels; First Series*, edited by Philip Schaff, fifth printing. Peabody, MA: Hendrickson Publishers, 2012.

———. *Ancient Christian Commentary on Scripture: New Testament Ia; Matthew 1-13*. Edited by Manlio Simonetti. Downers Grove, IL: InterVarsity Press, 2001.

Basil the Great. "The Hexaemeron." In *Nicene and Post-Nicene Fathers. Vol. 8. Basil: Letters and Selected Works; Second Series*, edited by Philip Schaff and Henry Wave, fifth printing. Peabody, MA: Hendrickson, 2012.

———. *On the Holy Spirit*. Edited and Introduction by Stephen Hildebrand. Popular Patristic Series. Yonkers, NY: St Vladimir's Seminary Press, 2011.

Chromatius. *Ancient Christian Commentary on Scripture: New Testament Ia; Matthew 1-13*. Edited by Manlio Simonetti. Downers Grove, IL: InterVarsity Press, 2001

Chrysostom. *Ancient Christian Commentary on Scripture: New Testament Ia; Matthew 1-13*. Edited by Manlio Simonetti. Downers Grove, IL: InterVarsity Press, 2001.

———. "Homily XV: Matt. V. 1,2." In *Nicene and Post-Nicene Fathers. Vol. 10. Chrysostom: Homilies on the Gospel of Saint Matthew; First Series*, edited by Philip Schaff, fifth printing. Peabody, MA: Hendrickson, 2012.

Gregory of Nyssa. *The Life of Moses*. Translation and Introduction by Everett Ferguson and Abraham J. Malherbe. Preface by John Meyendorff. The Classics of Western Spirituality. Mahwah, New York: Paulist Press, 1978.

———. *The Lord's Prayer, The Beatitudes*. Translated by Hilda C. Graef. Vol 18. Ancient Christian Writers: The Works of the Fathers in Translation. Edited by Johannes Quasten and Joseph C. Plumpe. New York: Paulist Press, 1954.

Hamm, Dennis. *The Beatitudes in Context: What Luke and Matthew Meant*. Edited by Mary Ann Getty.

Zacchaeus Studies: New Testament. Wilmington, Delaware: Michael Glaziar, 1990.

Hierotheos, Metropolitan of Nafpaktos. *The Illness and Cure of the Soul in the Orthodox Tradition*. Revised Second Edition. Translated by Effie Mavromichali. Levadia, Greece: Birth of the Theotokos Monastery, 2010.

Hilary. *Ancient Christian Commentary on Scripture: New Testament Ia; Matthew 1-13*. Edited by Manlio Simonetti. Downers Grove, IL: InterVarsity Press, 2001.

Jerome. *Ancient Christian Commentary on Scripture: New Testament Ia; Matthew 1-13*. Edited by Manlio Simonetti. Downers Grove, IL: InterVarsity Press, 2001.

Kelly, J. N. D. *Early Christian Doctrines*. Revised Edition. New York, NY: HarperCollins, 1978.

Kodell, Jerome. *The Eucharist in the New Testament*. Zacchaeus Studies: New Testament, edited by Mary Ann Getty. Collegeville, MN: The Liturgical Press, 1988.

Lossky, Vladimir. *Dogmatic Theology: Creation, God's Image in Man, & the Redeeming Work of the Trinity*. A Revised, Annotated, and Expanded Second Edition of *Theologie dogmatique*. Edited by Olivier Clement and Michel Stavrou. Translated by Anthony P.

Gythiel. Yonkers, NY: Saint Vladimir's Seminary Press, 2017.

———. *In the Image and Likeness of God*. Edited by John H. Erickson and Thomas E. Bird. Introduction by. John Meyendorff. Crestwood, NY: St Vladimir's Press, 1974.

———. *The Mystical Theology of the Eastern Church*. Crestwood, NY: St Vladimir's Press, [1957?].

———. *Orthodox Theology: An Introduction*. Translated by Ian and Ihita Kesarcodi-Watson. Crestwood, NY: St Vladimir's Press, 1978.

Meyendorff, John. *St. Gregory Palamas and Orthodox Spirituality*. Translated by Adele Fiske. Crestwood, NY: St. Vladimir's Seminary Press, 1974.

Meyendorff, Paul. *The Anointing of the Sick*. Book I of the Orthodox Liturgy Series. Crestwood, NY: St. Vladimir's Seminary Press, 2009.

Patsavos, Lewis. *Spiritual Dimensions of the Holy Canons*. Brookline, MA: Holy Cross Orthodox Press, 2003.

Russell, Norman. *Fellow Workers with God: Orthodox Thinking on Theosis*. Book 5 of the Foundations Series. Crestwood, NY: St. Vladimir's Seminary Press, 2009.

Saliba, Metropolitan Philip (Saliba) and Joseph Allen. *Meeting the Incarnate God: From the Human Depths to the Mystery of Fidelity*. Brookline, MA: Holy Cross Orthodox Press, 2009.

Alexander Schmemann. *Introduction to Liturgical Theology*. Translated by Ashleigh E. Moorehouse. Crestwood, NY: St. Vladimir's Seminary Press, 1966.

Stavropoulos, Archimandrite Christoforos. *Partakers of Divine Nature*. Translated by Rev. Stanley Harakas. Sixth printing. Minneapolis: Light and Life Publishing, 1976.

Tarazi, Paul Nadim. *The New Testament: Introduction; Volume 3; Johannine Writings*. Crestwood, NY: St. Vladimir's Seminary Press, 2004.

Venianmin, Christopher. *The Orthodox Understanding of Salvation: "Theosis" in Scripture and Tradition*. Dalton, PA: Mount Thabor, 2016.

Ware, Timothy (Bishop Kallistos of Diokleia). *The Orthodox Church*, New Edition. London: Penguin Books, 1997.

Book Endorsements

To be blessed ourselves, God has to be in us. Deacon Christopher Mertens uses some of the best of the Church's mystical tradition to demonstrate how we share in God's blessedness. He concisely shows how the Beatitudes are foundational to the New Covenant, and how Christ serves as the "new Moses" in bringing people into communion with God. This book is for those who, having been introduced to the Church's Tradition, desire to delve further into their life in Christ. Pastors will also find the work beneficial for straightforwardly instructing their parishioners. Deacon Christopher's work is well worth the read.

> — Bishop Thomas Joseph
>   Diocese of Oakland, Charleston, and the Mid-Atlantic, Antiochian Orthodox Christian Archdiocese of North America
> — Rev. Father James Purdie
>   Pastor of Saint Basil the Great Orthodox Christian Church, Hampton, Virginia

I would like to congratulate Dn. Christopher J. Mertens for publishing his Master thesis in Applied Orthodox theology, titled: "The Beatitudes: A Pathway to Theosis." In his thesis, Dn. Christopher gives a full account of the sermon on the mount, delivered by our Lord Jesus Christ, whose authority is greater than that of Moses, for He proclaims the new Torah, the spiritual Covenant. In the Beatitudes, Jesus describes the way of true discipleship, of the character of those who are worthy to be called children of God, and of the manner of ascending a ladder which leads to theosis. On behalf of the faculty of the Antiochian House of Studies, I commend Dn. Christopher for his work, hoping that his thesis will imbue the reader with spiritual benefits.

> — V. Rev. Father Michel Najim (Th.D)
> President of the Antiochian House of Studies, La Verne, California

While there are a great many books dealing with the subject of Theosis at the level of dogmatic and mystical theology, including its elucidation in the fathers and grounding in the Scriptures, Mertens here provides a different approach. Through the interpretive lens of Gregory of Nyssa and other fathers, he utilizes Christ's own homiletic approach in the Sermon on the Mount to provide a 'way in' which connects the mystical life of the church to the life of the faithful within the world. The Beatitudes are here seen to be not simply moral imperatives or a virtue list but a means of spiritual ascent. The means of participation in the divine life described by the Beatitudes form a ladder stretching from earth to heaven and from this age to the eternal age to come.

> — Rev. Father Stephen De Young (Ph.D)
> Pastor of Archangel Gabriel Orthodox Church, Lafayette, Louisiana

No journey is as difficult as the one we make towards God and His blessedness. Yet, no journey has been so well-prepared and well-furnished. Fr. Deacon Christopher Mertens offers a wealth of material both in understanding as well as application in his study of the Beatitudes. Readers will appreciate what is offered to them, the treasures both new and old, of the Kingdom of God.

> — V. Rev. Father Stephen Freeman
> Pastor of Saint Anne Orthodox Church, Knoxville / Oak Ridge, Tennessee

Uitgeverij Orthodox Logos

- *De Orthodoxe Kerk: Verleden en heden* – Jean Meyendorff
- *Biecht en communie* – Alexander Schmemann
- *Verliefd Zijn op het Leven* – Samensteller: Maxim Hodak
- *De Orthodoxe Kerk* – Aartspriester Sergei Hackel
- *De mensenrechten in het licht van het Evangelie* – Nicolas Lossky
- *Geboren in Haat Herboren in Liefde* – Klaus Kenneth
- *Hegoumena Thaissia van Leouchino: brieven aan een novice*
- *Het Jezusgebed* – Een monnik van de oosterse kerk
- *Gebedenboek Voor Kinderen: Volgens De Orthodox Christelijke Traditie*
- *Dagboek Van Keizerin Alexandra* – Keizerin Alexandra
- *Mijn ontmoeting met Archimandriet Sophrony* – Aartspriester Silouan Osseel
- *Stap voor stap veranderen* – Vader Meletios Webber
- *De Weg Naar Binnen* – Metropoliet Anthony (Bloom) Van Sourozh
- *Geraakt door God's liefde* – Klooster van de Levenschenkende Bron Chania
- *De Heilige Silouan de Athoniet* – Archimandrite Sophrony
- *The Beatitudes: A Pathway to Theosis* – Christopher J. Mertens
- *De Kracht van de Naam* – Metropoliet Kallistos van Diokleia
- *De Orthodoxe Weg* – Metropoliet Kallistos van Diokleia
- *Serafim Van Sarov* – Irina Goraïnoff
- *Feesten van de Orthodoxe Kerk – een Leerzaam Kleurboek*
- *Catechetisch woord Over Het gebed van het Hart* – Aartspreiester Silouan Osseel
- *Naar de Eenheid?* – Leonide Ouspensky
- *Bidden Met Ikonen* – Jim Forest
- *Onze Gedachten Bepalen Ons Leven* – Vader Thaddeus Van Vitovnica
- *Alledaagse Heiligen En Andere Verhalen* – Archimandriet Tichon (Sjevkoenov)
- *Geestelijke Brieven* – Vader Jozef De Hesychast
- *Nihilisme* – Vader Serafim Rose
- *Gods Openbaring Aan Het Menselijk Hart* – Vader Serafim Rose
- *In De Kaukazus* – Monnik Merkurius
- *Terugkeer* – Archimandriet Nektarios Antonopoulos
- *Weest ook gij uitgebreid* – Archimandriet Zacharias (Zacharou)

- *Our Orthodox Holy Family* – Deacon David Lochbihler, J.D.
- *Prayers to Our Lady East and West* – Deacon David Lochbihler, J.D.
- *The Joy of Orthodoxy* – Deacon David Lochbihler, J.D.
- *The Inner Cohesion between the Bible and the Fathers in Byzantine Tradition* – S.M. Roye
- *St. Germanus of Auxerre* – Howard Huws
- *Elder Anthimos Of Saint Anne's* – Dr. Charalambos M. Bousias
- *Orthodox Preaching as the Oral Icon of Christ* – James Kenneth Hamrick
- *The Final Kingdom* – Pyotr Volkov

www.ingramcontent.com/pod-product-compliance
Lightning Source LLC
Chambersburg PA
CBHW020105240426
43661CB00002B/41